MONEY
in your
MAILBOX

MONEY
in your
MAILBOX:

How to start and operate
a mail order business

L. Perry Wilbur

THE WILEY PRESS
John Wiley & Sons, Inc
New York • Chichester • Brisbane • Toronto • Singapore

Library of Congress Cataloging in Publication Data

Wilbur, L. Perry.
  Money in your mailbox.

  Reprint. Originally published: Reston, Va.,: Reston
Pub. Co., c1979.
  Bibliography: p.
  Includes index.
  1. Mail-order business. 2. Advertising, Direct-mail.
3. Self-employed. I. Title.
[HF5466.W48 1985]   658.8'72   84-29192
ISBN 0-471-82586-7 (pbk.)

Printed in the United States of America

10

Contents

Preface

Ever wonder what it's like to find money in your mailbox day after day? Have you ever thought about starting a mail-order company through which you could launch a product or service and build a profitable business of your own—either part-time or full-time? If so, then this book is for you.

I started and operated a mail-order company of my own in preparation for writing this book, so much of the material is based on my actual experience. I'll never forget the thrill of seeing the first cash orders in my mailbox. I know that by following the guidelines in this book you will be able to experience the same thrill.

In the following pages you'll discover that there's no business like the mail-order business. In mail-order you're the boss. You can live anywhere you like and operate the business while holding down a regular job. You can start your business with limited funds and grow at whatever rate you think best.

All types of people can be found making good money in the mail-order business—single individuals, couples, families, students, retired people, moonlighters, working wives, or just about anyone who wants a profitable sideline. Many companies, both small and large, have set up mail-order divisions in order to capitalize on the money that can be made by mail.

Mail order could open the doors of the good life for you. At the very least, the mail-order business is a proven way to a second income and a bank account that just keeps on growing. At the very best, the business can provide much more than a second income. The mail-order industry is famous for its millionaire success stories.

You may never make a million dollars by running a mail-order company, but you can take in more money than you might expect—maybe more than you ever dreamed. You can become part of an amazing industry, one that has often been called the last frontier of fortune building.

I know there's a rewarding place for you in this exciting business. This book is meant to help you get started and to guide you in the operation of your company. Refer to it often as you build your business.

Welcome to the stimulating and unique world of mail order. May your profits be large and your mailbox overflow with cash orders.

L. PERRY WILBUR

MONEY
in your
MAILBOX

Part I

GETTING STARTED IN MAIL ORDER

SUCCESS STORY:
Thomas Hall Reports

Years ago, Thomas Hall visited Japan and liked it so much that he decided to run his business from there. He built a very profitable business by advertising and selling a variety of reports for consumers and businesses. One of his reports—on the subject of beauty—contained a number of beauty secrets and had great appeal for women everywhere.

Some of his reports sell for $50 and more, and Hall has sold them to mail-order customers all over the globe. One of his products is a guide on how to make a lot of money as a creator and seller of reports.

Hall is a highly successful mail-order operator whose products have strong appeal for people in all walks of life. He uses both ads and direct mail to reach customers.

1

A Mail-Order Business of Your Own

You in the mail-order business? Why not? There are numerous reasons why you should at least consider the idea. A mail-order business of your own can provide either an ideal leisure-time activity or an excellent business opportunity. A mail-order business offers a high profit potential and can generate a very substantial additional income. Many mail-order businesses take only a few hours a day to run. A lot of firms in business today are owned and operated by one person working alone. You'd be surprised how prosperous most of the established firms are.

Look at the facts. The *Wall Street Journal* estimates the total annual revenue from mail order at between $52 and $60 billion. That's a lot of money winging its way through the mails in this country. Why can't you get in on some of the action? Do people really buy this much by mail? You'd better believe they do, and they are going to be buying even more in the years to come.

Can anyone get into mail order? Yes. Just about anyone can get into the business. Of course, your chances for real success and big profits are much better if you have a few of the qualities that are most helpful in the business. In the words of the Department of Commerce, "In mail-order work, anyone with imagination, determination, and a willingness to study and experiment may have very little difficulty getting started. A number of the most successful one-man operations obtain an income as high as $40,000 to $50,000 a year." Many part-time firms take in from $6,000 to $20,000.

Total mail-order business is expected to double in size in the next several years. Why the big boom? Well, one reason is that more people are moving from the cities to the suburbs. Many Americans are getting fed up with the lack of service characteristic of so many stores today. Millions of buyers are, therefore, sending in their orders by mail. Shopping by mail saves them time, trouble, and usually money too.

Another more or less psychological reason why people do business by mail is that they enjoy anticipating the arrival of their purchases. It gives them a pleasant feeling to know their order is on the way, perhaps even a sense of mystery is involved.

WHAT TO SELL BY MAIL

Okay. Granted there's a prosperous future ahead, at least for the wise mail-order dealers who choose the right products and services to offer. But how does a newcomer like yourself decide on what to sell by mail?

The best answer to this key question is to be a copycat. That's right. In the mail-order business it's far wiser to offer a product that's already being sold successfully through the mail. Address labels, printing services, books, correspondence courses, information, health foods, religious materials, clothing products, foot-care materials, and many other product categories are all time-tested and being sold successfully by mail today. It's best to avoid starting a new and untested product or service until you learn more about the business and gain some helpful experience. You can always originate new products later, after you have learned how to test them and have mastered the fine points of launching a new product. In the beginning it's best to stick with proven sellers. See chapter 4, *Choosing Your Product or Service*.

Some of the best ideas for products can be picked up by browsing through the pages of some leading mail-order publications. Just a few of the many products advertised recently included a music scroll, a portable dishwasher, an exerciser, a family tree book and chart, a dog bed, an oxygen inhaler, a coat of arms emblem, a personalized rubber stamp, a vast assortment of how-to-do-it books, a secret money belt, rapid reading records, and reading glasses. All of these products are evidently selling. If the products weren't selling, you can bet that these mail-order companies would discontinue them.

What do most of these successful mail-order products have in common? The first thing you notice is that they're all a bit unusual. Most of the offerings have unique or otherwise attractive features. Many are items or products that you can't buy just anywhere. Many mail-order products are sold exclusively through the mail. If the customer wants the particular product advertised, he or she may have no choice but to purchase it from the company selling it by mail—a most enviable situation for the dealer.

Other attractions of successful mail-order products include price advantage, personalization, and, especially with novelty products, uniqueness. The key to success in mail order is, of course, the product. Select a product that people need or will want, and you're halfway home to good profits.

There are two basic ways to obtain the products you sell by mail. One very popular arrangement is to have various suppliers and companies drop-ship a product or products to your customers. In most drop-shipping arrangements you send your customer's order to your supplier, along with a shipping label addressed to your customer under your own company name. Your supplier then fills the order using your shipping label. This way you avoid having to keep a stock of the product on hand. The companies that drop-ship for you offer a special drop-ship price to you as their dealer. The difference between the retail price and the special drop-ship price is where you make your profit. Basically, you are supplying the customer order and the drop-ship company is supplying the product for you.

The second method is to keep the product on hand yourself. The problems with this method usually come from the need to calculate in advance how much stock to keep. You can't be sure how many orders you might receive. Either too much stock or too little can create problems. If possible, it's a good idea to try out both methods in a limited way until you decide which you like best.

WAYS TO GET MAIL-ORDER CUSTOMERS

How does a mail-order business owner get his or her customers? There are a number of ways, but, if you decide to try mail order part-time, the best way is to get your first orders by advertising. Does this mean that you have to understand advertising and place your own ads? Well, you do need to know the basics, but these can be mastered quickly. You'll need to know what goes into a pulling ad,

good idea to contact your printer in advance and let him know when he can expect to receive it. This advance notice isn't necessary for small orders.

Some mail-order operators phone their big orders in to the printer. This way their printer can plan his work. When printers are told to be ready for upcoming orders, it can be a great help and time-saver for both you and your printer. Printers like to plan their work schedule ahead, so they can get orders out as quickly and efficiently as possible.

You don't have to understand a lot of technical printing terms in order to obtain quality work. It does help, however, if you can talk to your printer in person. You can then explain to him just what you want done on any special orders.

Offset Printing

Most of the printing done in mail order today is called *offset*. As a mail-order operator, you take or send your material (to be printed) to a printer in camera-ready form. This means that whatever you wish to be printed must be ready to be photographed by your printer. After the photograph has been taken, an offset plate is made from the photo negative. Your printer can then turn out any number of copies you want.

Your sales letters, circulars, and order forms can be printed by offset, but it's usually better to have your business letterheads done by letterpress (a form of printing using actual type).

Special Printing Orders

You may occasionally have a special form, insert, circular, or flat-sheet (a single sheet of copy you want duplicated) to be printed. Ask your printer how quickly such orders can be filled, for there will be times when you suddenly realize that you need copies of a new form or a special circular.

Check over your supplies now and then to avoid running out of reply envelopes, sales letters, order forms, or circulars when you need them most. Be sure to submit refill orders long before your present supply is exhausted.

Payment for Printing Orders

Practically all printers expect payment in full with each printing order you send them. On the other hand, if you stick with one printing firm and give it a large amount of business over a period of time, it's quite possible that the firm will grant you credit and allow you to make a downpayment on your printing order with the balance due when it is filled and shipped back to you.

It's also true that you can get to know a printer very well if you see and deal with him or her on a personal basis. In time, you might come to trust each other so that a credit arrangement could be worked out.

Backup Printers

One good way to insure that you always have access to quality printers is to use an out-of-town printer as a backup. This way you can be virtually certain that you can get action on your printing orders regardless of circumstances.

Printers Are Competitive

Something else to remember about printers is that they're generally competitive. In other words, one printer may do your order for you for less money than another. It will pay you to shop around and compare prices before you decide to give your business to any one printer. For example, a mail-order printer may do the work cheaper and just as effectively as a local company.

Get on the Mailing Lists of Printers

One benefit of writing to a number of printers is that many of them will put your name on their mailing lists. This means that you'll be sure to hear about special orders, co-op printing deals, price-cuts, copy preparation information, and the like. Printers may also obtain your name and address from the printing firm you deal with and put you on their own mailing lists. This is a good way for you to find new printers.

Some Suggested Printers

You should select your own printer after checking him out and possibly testing the quality of his work with an order. But you might find the following suggested printers helpful. At one time or another, I have used some of these printers in my own business. I found them to be helpful, reliable, and businesslike. Their prices were, in most cases, reasonable, and the quality of their work was good.

Keep in mind that printers, like other companies, do change their location from time to time. The addresses given for these printers are correct at this writing, but they could well change.

- Paducah Printing Company
  8th and Monroe
  Paducah, Kentucky

- American Speedy Printing Centers
  6720 Arlington Expressway
  Jacksonville, Florida 32211

- John Blair Printing Company
  22 Davis Street
  Harrison, New Jersey 07029

- Champion Printing Company
  Box 148
  Ross, Ohio 45061

SOURCES OF ADDITIONAL HELP

Before you launch your company, you might wish to contact the following sources for additional help and guidance. Ask them to send you their free folders and pamphlets on mail order. There may be a small charge for certain folders, but most are still free at this writing. Request them soon, in case their supplies are limited. These folders may not be available at a later date, and the current addresses might also be subject to change. Here are the addresses:

- Small Business Administration
  1441 L Street, N. W.
  Washington, D.C. 20416

  Ask for the pamphlet on "Selling by Mail Order."

- Superintendent of Documents
  U.S. Government Printing Office
  Washington, D.C. 20402

  Request a copy of "Guides Against Deceptive Ads."

• Council of Better Business Bureaus
1515 Wilson Blvd.
Washington, D.C. 20036

Ask for their free folder, "Tips on Mail-Order Profit Mirages." You might also request the pamphlet entitled "Code of Advertising." There may be a small charge for it.

• American Entrepreneurs'
Association
2311 Pontius Ave.
Los Angeles, California 90064

If you like the sound of this business and can see yourself in it part-time, by all means read more about it. Your library will have a number of good books on the business, and several known mail-order publications offer inexpensive booklets on how to actually start your own company. *House Beautiful Magazine* is one of these. The Small Business Administration can also send you information. It's a good idea to write to these sources and request information.

The best way to really learn the business is to actually get into it. Send your order to a printer for professional letterheads, along with regular business and return envelopes. Then you can start communicating in a businesslike way. You can grow from that point forward, as you build a profitable mail-order company of your own.

SUCCESS STORY: John Bear

John Bear got into the mail-order business with a good idea: he decided to publish and advertise a report on how to get a college degree by mail. One of John's early ads cost him $120 and returned a gross of $7,000. His net profit turned out to be about $5,000. Delighted with his success in mail-order, Bear made some changes in his life: he left his job in Chicago and moved to northern California. He now runs his ad in over thirty leading mail-order publications and enjoys a handsome retirement income from his huge profits.

2
The Self-Employment Picture

MAIL ORDER IS SELF-EMPLOYMENT

Once you get your mail-order business launched, you will have joined the ranks of the self-employed. To be honest about it, there are two sides to the self-employment picture. There are both advantages and disadvantages to working for yourself. You need to be aware of both sides of the coin.

You'll have plenty of company on the day you start your mail-order business. The Small Business Administration says that 1,000 new businesses are started every day in the United States alone. Fifty percent of new businesses fail in the first two years. Eighty-five percent fail in the first five years. Not all of these new businesses are mail-order companies. But still, the number of new businesses of all types that fail is shockingly large.

WHY NEW BUSINESSES FAIL

The SBA says that there's one chance in five that a new business will still be operating under the original owner after a ten-year period. According to the SBA 92.1% of new business fail because of lack of management ability, 1.1% because of neglect, ⅓ of 1% for fraud, .6 because of disaster and the remaining 5.6% for unknown reasons.

Many self-employed people see their yearly incomes rise year after year. It takes hard work, of course, but the point is that nobody can step in and say you can't make any more money. Your salary can't be frozen, and nobody can beat you out of a promotion, because you're the boss. It's your company, your business.

Being Happy in Your Work

A major consideration that you shouldn't overlook is job contentment. Would you be happier working for yourself than for someone else? Dr. Karl Menninger has stated that three-fourths of psychiatric patients suffer from dissatisfaction in their work.

Another serious question related to job contentment is the question of whether you can make progress in your job. Ask yourself what type of work you can advance in most quickly—working for some company or for yourself. Bear in mind that although self-employment may be tough going until you are established, it's very possible to reap a rich harvest, eventually making far more than you could ever earn with an employer.

Let's face it. The name of the game today is progress. Everybody and his brother wants to move up the success ladder. Your work years will go by fast. If you don't move up, or if you get stuck someplace in the climb, you may not have long to enjoy the so-called good life.

You See the Direct Results of Your Efforts

How about the chance to see the direct results of your own efforts? This possibility alone draws many into self-employment. The results of your planning and efforts are especially apparent in mail order. Come up with an attractive product or service, and you will quickly see the results. Your level of success will relate directly to your overall planning and advertising strategy.

SOME DISADVANTAGES OF SELF-EMPLOYMENT

Can You Make Decisions?

To understand both sides of the picture, you need to be aware of some aspects of self-employment that might trip you up. One possible pitfall is found in the decision-making process itself.

Can you make decisions? Is it easy or agonizing for you to make important decisions? Do you put off making decisions whenever possible? You must answer these questions honestly when you consider launching your own business. Once you get into business, nobody will be there to make the many needed decisions for you. The way you handle decisions will determine whether you sink or swim. If you do find it difficult to make sound decisions, you should probably forget starting your own business.

The right decisions are very vital to the growth of a new business. Make the wrong decisions, and you alone are the villain. Still, keep in mind that you can't determine the overall quality of your judgment until you begin to use it and actually start making business decisions.

The Risk of Going into Debt

Another worrisome aspect of self-employment is the inescapable fact that most self-employed people are forced to go into debt. It may take some time to become established in mail order or any other new business. During this period you will have to make some sacrifices in the area of financial security. Millions find it tough to give up the peace of mind that security assures you. You won't be able to be sure about your life-style until you've managed to become established.

On the other hand, a great many who launch a mail-order business do so on a part-time basis. It's possible to hold down a regular job and still run a mail-order company. I've done it myself. Running a mail-order company can take anywhere from a few hours a day up to over forty hours a week. It all depends on the size and scope of your business. The time involved will also depend on how slowly or quickly you wish to grow. You will almost certainly start small and grow slowly. So you could be in mail order with a commitment of only a few hours a day.

Good Health Is a Must

Generally speaking, good health is important for success in self-employment. You could be financially wiped out, should you lose your health while self-employed. As the boss, if you miss a few days or weeks, you can get behind quickly and go down the drain. Handicapped people, however, have managed to run mail-order companies and have turned a handsome profit doing it. It depends on the person and his or her total abilities.

Keeping Up with Changes in Your Field

When you're not actually on the job, running your business, much of your free time will have to be spent keeping up with the changing state of the business. There's a real need to stay well informed on all changing developments in postal rates and laws, product information, taxes, and the various other aspects of the mail-order business. You'll want to know, too, what other products and services are being offered and how well they seem to be doing. This means devoting time to research.

An Extra Work Day Each Week

One fact that discourages millions of people is that self-employed workers spend more time on the job (one day extra each week, according to a government study) than those who are not self-employed. With many workers looking forward to the four-day work week, this extra day of work appears to many to be too big a sacrifice. But, as already pointed out, a mail-order business need not take this much time at all, at least not until it has grown by leaps and bounds. At that point, you'll probably be making enough money so that you'll be able to hire others to handle the extra workload. Besides, when you're working on a winner you probably won't mind putting in a little extra time yourself.

Perhaps it is because success as a self-employed person requires a healthy amount of hard work, good luck, sound judgment, and persistence that only one-tenth of all who work for a living actually work for themselves. Many try self-employment for a time, but find that they lack the skills or abilities needed in the business selected. So they return to work for somebody else.

HOW MANY PEOPLE ARE SELF-EMPLOYED?

Of the seven million self-employed people in the United States, half are professional people—doctors, lawyers, dentists, and the like. One-fourth of the self-employed are independent farmers. The rest of the seven million operate small businesses such as motels, groceries, gas stations, retail establishments, museums, and various consumer-type stores. Many people are self employed because they have few other choices. Many have no clearly defined skills that can be marketed profitably to a prospective employer.

CONCLUSIONS ABOUT SELF-EMPLOYMENT

Even though success cannot be assured, millions of people the world over work for themselves and wouldn't have it any other way. Wherever one lives, there's something inviting and highly stimulating about waking up each morning and knowing that you're the one in charge of yourself and your work. That's freedom! And it's most satisfying.

Part of the joy of working for yourself, aside from the unlimited possibilities, is the knowledge that you're in control of your work and, to a large extent, your destiny. As a mail-order operator and self-employed writer, I can vouch for this truth.

Since launching my own mail-order business several years ago and joining the ranks of free-lance writers years earlier, I've come alive as never before. I'm anxious to start work each morning. The reason is that I like my work. It is work that interests me tremendously. I choose the products and services I will offer and the publications in which I will run my ads. I am able to select the publications I will write for and the subjects I'll write about. I work at my own pace and can usually work on my writing assignments anywhere I like. I also get to travel some, gathering material and doing interviews.

A few years ago, Sheryl Bodily, of Columbia Falls, Montana, became a self-employed professional artist. He decided to leave the security of a steady job and try his luck as an artist. He had worked part-time at his painting for ten years, while working full-time at a local sawmill. After ten years he decided that he was good enough to support his wife and six children by the sale of his artwork alone. He proved he was right.

Bodily's paintings—most of which depict western scenes or the activities of Indians—are now widely acclaimed. His first exhibit was in Hungry Horse, Montana. Since that day, other work from his brush has been displayed throughout the United States.

Today there's an eager market for Bodily's work, because he believed that he could make it in self-employment and took the plunge. By taking the plunge and launching your own mail-order company, you may well be taking the most important career step of your life. Think well on it.

In summary, before you decide to join the ranks of the self-employed, be sure to consider the following points:

1. Most new businesses fail because of a lack of business knowledge and ability. Make it a point to find out as much as you

the catalog departments of both stores and mail-order firms, and the catalog desks of mail-order companies found in department stores.

Q. *How well have newcomers to mail order done with their first ads and products?*

A. A good example is John Sicher—he started in mail order by offering watches and calculators. He ran his first ad in thirty publications and his ad brought in an incredible 30,000 orders and a cash bonanza of over $600,000.

Q. *What are the most important elements for success in mail order?*

A. A good idea for a product or service and good judgment in advertising and selling that product or service.

CHOOSING A PRODUCT OR SERVICE

Q. *Are there any tips that might help me in coming up with a new product or service?*

A. A good idea for one person might be a poor idea for someone else, but here is a tip that could easily guide you to one or more fine product or service items: there's going to be a huge new interest in and respect for marriage in the closing decades of this century. Once again, it will be the "in thing" to be married. So you might start now to try to dream up, plan, and produce a product or service that would appeal to married couples everywhere. There will be millions of new marriages, and these new families will need and want all sorts of things. I'm working on this myself and am convinced that it will pay off handsomely.

Q. *Before investing time, money, and effort in producing a product for mail order, is there a way to judge the quality of what the competition is offering?*

A. Looking at the ads in leading mail-order publications will quickly tell you what's being offered. But you should do more than this. Order some mail-order products and look them over. If, for example, you're thinking of offering an informational booklet, you should send for similar booklets being sold and look them over carefully. See how they compare with yours in quality, price, usefulness, and overall value. You should also request details on various offers and study the sales letters and literature you receive.

Q. *Is a system for getting out of debt a good product to offer by mail?*

A. As long as there are people around, many of them are going to have trouble staying out of debt. According to research figures, more than one million unpaid bills are abandoned every month by people who just move out of town without leaving a forwarding address. Eleven million bad checks also turn up each month. Materials, manuals, and booklets offering a solution to debt are already being sold by mail, but there's plenty of room for new offers. Your own system may be much better than the plans now being sold—your plan may be more helpful, more informative, or more attractive in price.

Q. *With today's increase in violence, would a self-defense product be right for mail order?*

A. Yes. Many self-defense products have been sold by mail for years. Millions of people continue to live in fear, so the market for such items is still large. A recent ad states that a tear gas device called the "paralyzer" can earn $20,000 to $50,000 per year for a distributor.

Q. *Wouldn't selling full-length books by mail, and not just short booklets, be a good way to go in mail-order?*

A. Actually, more books are reportedly being sold via mail-order than in all the nation's bookstores combined (according to *Publishers Weekly*). The big catalog houses that sell to millions of buyer-customers often include at least a few full-length books for sale. There are numerous other smaller companies including those that offer full-length books alone on every conceivable subject. This could be a good route for you a bit later, after you've gained some experience.

Q. *Can a correspondence course be too complicated and expensive to produce and sell by mail?*

A. Yes. I recommend that you wait until you've had some experience in mail order and had some success with less complicated offers before trying to sell a correspondence course. Film star Mickey Rooney recently told the press that he planned to leave show business and devote his time to marketing a self-study acting course he's been working on for fifteen years. This is a good idea, and such a course ought to sell with Rooney's name behind it. But the long time that Rooney has spent on developing his course shows how involved some courses can be. So

SUCCESS STORY: Writers' Consultation and Placement Service

Former teachers, secretaries, bankers, and others are doing well by offering either part- or full-time writers' consultation services by mail. The writing consultation may range from poems or short stories to articles, booklets, and even full-length books. Fees run from around ten or twenty dollars to hundreds of dollars. Some of these mail services provide criticism of the writing and give hints and directions on how the material may be improved. Other services charge a set fee to place material with newspapers, magazines, or book publishers.

One enterprising woman in New England thought of the idea of operating a colony for writers. She ran a small display ad in several magazines for writers. She has done this for years and also offers consultation and instructional booklets by mail.

4
Choosing Your Product or Service

HOW MAIL ORDER WORKS

Success in mail order often follows a simple pattern. First, a need for a certain product is discovered, and an item is developed and produced to meet that need. Next, the product is tested with a few initial ads offering real value for the buyer's money. The orders received are filled efficiently and promptly. Finally, the business is expanded by increasing the amount of money devoted to advertising. If handled wisely, the increased advertising will bring in a growing number of orders.

The entire idea of a mail-order business might be summed up this way: first, you obtain or originate a product or service to sell; second, you must reach prospective customers with information about your product. That's mail order in a nutshell.

WHY DO PEOPLE BUY BY MAIL?

Why do they do it? Why do more and more people send cash, checks, and money orders through the mail for all manner of products and services? There are a variety of reasons, and as the operator of your own mail-order business, you should be aware of them.

Convenience

One big reason for buying by mail is convenience. Many stores today seem to care little about a customer's business. In a great many stores today customers are left to wait on themselves. Service is a thing of the past. If you find what you want, that's fine. If you don't, tough luck! That seems to be the attitude of many stores. Times have changed. You might say that the customer is no longer right—at least in many stores. Shopping by mail eliminates the need to scour a store in search of needed items.

The Freedom of Ordering by Mail

A person who shops by mail often achieves a sense of freedom. No confrontation with a salesman is necessary. The sales talk is in the ad or in the sales literature received by mail. It can be tossed in the wastebasket or set aside for later consideration. It can also be acted upon at once.

The higher-priced products in stores are usually kept under the watchful eye of a salesperson hoping to motivate the customer to take action. Not so with mail order. A buyer is free to decide to buy or not in the comfort and privacy of his or her own home or apartment. That's freedom—without pressure of any kind.

It Saves Time and Parking Problems

Another reason for mail-order buying, similar to the two already named, is that buying by mail saves time that would otherwise be spent fighting traffic and coping with parking problems. It's true that many large shopping malls have solved the parking problem to a large extent, but a shopper may want to visit one or more stores not located in a mall. In addition, the malls get terribly crowded on weekends and during holiday periods. Accidents can and do take place, just getting in and out of these huge parking areas.

To Take Advantage of Bargains

Retailers have been using the lure of the bargain for years. The chance to save money has pulling power just about everywhere. This lure works wonders in the mail-order business, depending, of course, on what the bargain happens to be. One example is a booklet advertised as "revealing the secrets of a long and healthy life." The asking price was only one dollar. This offer obviously looked like a bargain to many buyers and no doubt did well for the seller.

Another bargain offer advertised recently was the chance to hear again many of the old favorite radio programs and stars of yesteryear. About fifteen hundred different programs were available on cassettes, tape reels, and cartridges. The price quoted for a catalog listing the programs was two dollars. A strong interest in Depression Era nostalgia items at the time of the offer naturally added to its appeal.

Impulse Buying

Up to a certain price threshold level, impulse buying is an important factor in mail order. The temptation to buy may not be as strong as when a customer is actually in a store and looking at a product, trying it on, admiring it, or whatever. But display ads often show attractive pictures of a product. A well done display ad can often stimulate a customer's impulse to buy.

Maybe some buyers have just had a bad day, like the sound of the offer, or just want to buy a given item. Let's face it. If people will plunk down cash to buy an impulse item like the book filled with blank pages called *The Nothing Book*, they will buy almost anything. At this writing, several hundred thousand copies of *The Nothing Book* have been sold. People everywhere often buy a few things just to give themselves a lift. There's no question about it. Impulse buying is here to stay. It goes on in stores every day. And it also brings in orders by mail.

Special Attractions of the Product

A good example of a special-attraction item is one offered by a company in Tennessee. They are currently advertising and selling wallpaper with over thirty etchings from the boyhood and rise to stardom of Elvis Presley. The wallpaper comes in six colors.

Whether sold in a store, by mail, or both ways, you can clearly see the special attraction of such a product. Product items with a connection to superstars who die have always sold well and will continue to sell.

The Fun of Anticipating Its Arrival

Another key reason why so many people buy by mail is they get a kick out of anticipating the arrival of the item in the mail. It comes addressed to the buyer, so it seems very personal. The buyer can await its arrival with real expectation, a certain amount of excitement, and maybe even a sense of mystery.

It's plain fun to receive things in the mail. It's also true that many people don't get much mail. The arrival of their order can grow in importance during the time it takes to be shipped and actually received. For many lonely people, the arrival of an anticipated package may well be an event that gives the buyer a badly needed lift and feeling of pleasure.

The Psychological Appeal of Newness

There are two schools of thought about mail-order products. Some so-called experts recommend that newcomers offer a product that is already being sold with success by other mail-order operators. Others believe that newcomers might well do better by offering something new.

The number of orders you receive is certainly going to be greatly reduced if dozens of other mail-order operators are offering the same product or item. It used to confuse me when I read in various mail-order instruction materials that the way to proceed was to be a copycat and sell the same items already being offered. I believe the copycat idea is true to a certain degree, but success often depends on what the product actually is and how many others are selling it.

I can tell you for certain, based on my own years of experience in mail order, that some of the items I offered that were also being sold by others proved to be complete duds. I ran good ads for these items in leading mail-order magazines and weekly tabloids, but too many others were selling the same thing or something very similar.

I still remember looking at one of my ads in a weekly tabloid, and in the same classified section I counted almost a dozen other ads offering the same basic product (a legal form). When the final results were in, the orders I received weren't enough to even pay for the ad.

So I advise you to take the idea of being a copycat with a grain of salt. It might work well for you at times, when not too many others are offering the same thing. But there's no guarantee that you're going to do well, just because others are selling the same item. The competition might very well hurt your own sales. You can, of course, test out any doubtful products or items first, to see if the market for them has already been tapped out by other mail-order operators.

It's good to remain a little skeptical in your reading about mail-order. All kinds of instruction courses and materials concerning mail order are being offered today. Some are good and worth the money; others are not based on real facts. Some of these plans for making money by mail just don't work, as I found out in my early experiences with buying and trying some of them.

On the other hand, there are some sound reasons for offering something new to prospects. New products and offers may be a little harder to introduce and establish, but many mail-order operators have done well with them over the years. Some of my own products were brand new, and they continue to sell for me.

Prospects like to buy and own something new. It's ingrained in most people. Part of the lift some people used to get from buying a new hat, when hats sold especially well, was the sheer newness of it. It gave them a happy feeling. There's something very basic about this appeal of newness. Why is it that countless millions of people tune in to radio and television news programs day after day? They may want to be informed, but they also crave the very newness of the daily news.

OTHER REASONS FOR BUYING BY MAIL

Along with the reasons for buying by mail already given, a few others are worth keeping in mind too. An important one is the buyer's belief that the product that he or she will be getting by mail will be of better quality than can be gotten locally.

Many buyers enjoy owning products that are different in some way or another. The novelty appeal of a number of mail-order products is very apparent. Back in the golden days of radio programs, I well remember sending in cereal box tops for special products like the Captain Midnight badge and secret decoder. Such highly prized items could only be obtained by mail order. They were unusual and exciting products. The days they arrived in the mail were special ones, especially if you were the first kid on the block to get one.

There's one type of mail-order buyer who has little choice but to do business by mail order. These buyers are the shut-ins. For many of the elderly, the handicapped, or those homebound for whatever reason, mail order is a real lifesaver. The products and services they need come right to their front doors and mailboxes, saving them considerable hardship.

THE DOMINANT WANTS OF PEOPLE

The reasons why people buy by mail can be traced to one or more of the dominant human wants or desires. Customers will not hesitate to order by mail to fulfill these different wants and desires. A mail-order product that satisfies one or more of these wants will be sought after and bought. The dominant wants of most people are:

- To enjoy oneself
- To be popular
- To be healthy
- To save time
- To escape physical pain
- To be clean
- To attract the opposite sex
- To make money
- To be praised
- To conserve possessions
- To satisfy one's appetite
- To be in style
- To avoid effort
- To save money
- To gratify curiosity
- To avoid trouble
- To be like others
- To avoid criticism
- To protect one's reputation
- To have beautiful possessions
- To be an individual
- To have security
- To be appreciated

- To take advantage of opportunities
- To be secure in buying
- To be important
- To be creative
- To be self-confident
- To be successful
- To have more leisure time
- To have influence over others

A mail-order product that fulfills a combination of these human wants will have a lot going for it. When deciding on a product to sell by mail, refer to this list of dominant human desires. A concentrated effort to center your product and your selling strategy around several of these mass desires will pay off handsomely. Run down the want list with your product or service. Does it fulfill any of these human desires? If so, how many? Will it sell year-round? For example, a huge industry is built around peoples' desire to have more romance in their lives. The large profits made year-round in the cosmetics industry is proof that millions of people want to look more attractive.

The Boom in Historical Romances

At this writing, historical romance novels are selling millions of copies. Romance books in general are chalking up new sales records. The reason is quite simple. Millions of people desire romance and will buy books and other products that offer it. Many such books are sold by mail to a seemingly endless market of buyers.

The Vitamin Industry

Another example of want-fulfillment is the vitamin industry. It now does over 300 million dollars worth of business a year and continues to grow. Why? Because millions of people have a strong, basic desire to maintain their health and vitality. Drive by almost any golf course on a nice day, and you'll see people out there playing golf. Many play golf simply because they love the game. But a large number play golf regularly simply because they want to have and maintain vim, vigor, and vitality. Maybe you can come up with a new product to appeal to these countless millions interested in keeping their health.

A FABULOUS MAIL-ORDER PRODUCT

Think what a four-star, fabulous mail-order product you would have if it related to all of the dominant wants of most people. Try to offer a product or service that will at least relate to two or three of the key human desires. For example, a product geared to the desire to make money might also include the desire for comfort and security.

Ask yourself how a product or service you're considering will make a buyer feel happier, more popular, better educated, more stylish, less tired, or what have you. Think about human needs and desires. And then try to match them with a product or service you can obtain or produce yourself. It's vital that you keep in mind the way that your chosen product meets these mass desires. When it comes time to plan your product's advertising or sales literature, this information will be very important.

It's the underlying meaning behind a product or service that often makes it irresistible. Take life insurance as an example. Few people want to buy more life insurance on any given day. But the wise person selling life insurance—whether by mail or face to face—talks about a secure and satisfying retirement income, a college education for a couple's children, a dream trip to Europe, a second home at the lake, and other tangible desires. These are the things a sound insurance program with a growing cash value over the years can make possible for the buyer. But the words "life insurance" turn many people off. The emphasis should be on the things that life insurance stands for and can make possible.

GET THE TOTAL MARKETING PICTURE

One objective of this book is to help you to see the total marketing picture of the product or service you choose to sell by mail. An understanding of the total marketing picture can considerably increase your chances of success in mail order, even if the product is your very first one.

By the total market picture, I mean packaging, advertising, promotion, merchandising, and selling. You will use advertising and promotion the most in mail order, but some knowledge of the other areas will certainly be of help.

Usually the more you know about your product the more you will sell of it. This is one good reason for originating or producing your mail-order product yourself. By creating it yourself, you will know it better than anyone else. And your special knowledge of it will aid you in advertising and promoting it.

ENTHUSIASM FOR YOUR PRODUCT

One of the first mail-order products that I originated was a book (really a minibook) on how to increase one's creative powers and abilities. I reasoned that this product related to several of the key human desires and could certainly be sold successfully by mail. After I completed the minibook, I discovered that it fulfilled several of the dominant wants:

- the desire to be more creative
- the desire for enjoyment
- the appeal of being an individual (which my product met in several ways)
- the desire to make money (a strong promise of the product)
- the desire to gratify curiosity
- the desire to take advantage of an opportunity
- the desire to increase self-confidence (through the act of creating things)
- the desire to express one's personality
- the desire to be an important person

A few of the other key desires were implied indirectly by my product.

So my original product related to about half of the basic human wants. This led me to have a number of copies of the minibook printed in order to meet the orders that came in after the first ads for the product appeared.

I'm happy to report that this minibook is still selling by mail today and has been one of my best products. I use both ads and direct mail to tell prospects about it. Some who have bought the minibook have even taken the time to write to me personally and praise the product. It has, in a number of cases, opened up a whole new way of life for the buyer. It has also added quite a bit to my bank account over the last several years.

I want to emphasize something here—enthusiasm for your product or service. Whatever you offer to buyers by mail, you'll need to be enthused about it. After planning and seeing my original minibook come to life following months of work and development, I found that I was filled with enthusiasm for it. My enthusiasm for the product was a great help in working out the ads, sales letters, and literature for it.

Don't try to offer something by mail that you don't believe in yourself, can't see the value of, or can't have genuine enthusiasm for. There is real power in enthusiasm. This power can serve as a foundation for your new and growing mail-order business.

START WITH ONE PRODUCT OR SERVICE

I found that one of the most important rules of the mail-order business is that a beginner should start with only one product or service. I can't emphasize this too much. You need to know a lot about the business before trying to sell several products simultaneously.

When you select your first product you want to aim for an item with a hobby or do-it-yourself appeal. Look for something that's different from what's being sold in stores. If you find a product within these guidelines you will be well on your way to a profitable start in mail order. The appendix at the end of this chapter will give you some ideas for products or services.

A specialty product is an item that is sold exclusively by the seller. A booklet that you produce, for example, or some other product that you originate and sell yourself would be considered a specialty product.

I did a lot of thinking about what I wanted to sell first. I wanted a simple product that I could have complete control over. I first considered selling a product manufactured by an established company, but I decided that I preferred handling my own item—something I could produce myself.

I studied a number of products that were being sold by mail. I did this by actually answering the ads for a variety of products. When I looked over the sales material and literature on these various offers, I was impressed by the number of informational booklets that were being sold by mail.

INFORMATIONAL BOOKLETS CONTINUE TO SELL

I did some more checking and discovered that informational booklets of all kinds form one of the main product categories of the mail-order industry. I noticed that ads for these booklets were appearing in most mail-order publications as far back as the 1940s and 1950s. They have continued to sell well in the 1980s, with every indication that they'll keep pulling in orders through the rest of the century.

An informational booklet seemed like a good item to start with. I felt certain I could put together one or more that would be helpful to many buyers.

I ordered a number of different booklets by mail, read them carefully, and thought about creating one of my own. In a few weeks, I was busy writing a booklet on the subject of success. I reasoned that a booklet on how to be more successful would appeal to many buyers and sell continually. After about a month's work, I had completed a booklet.

The information field is one of the largest individual phases of mail order. There are definite advantages in beginning with a product of this type. It's easy to get started with and is less of a gamble than most other types of offers. Little money is needed to start, and the chance for a high profit return is excellent.

A booklet that you create, have printed, and sell by mail does not have to be fancy looking at all. The buyer doesn't care what your booklet looks like as long as it's neat and readable. Length is not terribly important either. It's the information in the booklet that counts the most. That is what the buyer wants.

Should you like the idea of producing your own informational booklet as your first product item to sell, it will help you to refer to the following list of book topics that have long proven themselves to be consistent sellers.

1. Self-help
2. Moneymaking ideas
3. Business opportunities
4. The occult
5. Religion
6. Travel

HOW-TO-DO-IT BOOKLETS

Some of the best continuing sellers in the mail-order informational field are how-to-do-it booklets. There are bound to be at least a few such subjects that interest you or that you already know something about. With a little time and research, you can easily write up such a booklet. If you don't type, you could farm it out. After the pages have been neatly typed, the next step is to have enough copies of the booklet printed to fill the initial orders you'll receive.

There will always be buyers interested in the do-it-yourself approach. To stimulate your thinking along these lines, some how-to booklets currently being sold by mail include the following titles:

- How to Stop Smoking
- How to Become a Consultant
- How to Develop Psychic Powers
- How to Become a Coin Dealer
- How to Make Big Money in the Stock Market
- How to Write for Profit
- How to Operate a Charm and Modeling Business
- How to Open Locked Doors Instantly
- How to Raise Rabbits
- How to Lose Weight
- How to Stay Young
- How to Become a Piano Tuner

These are only a few of the hundreds of how-to-do-it booklets now being sold. The ads for many of them are continually seen in various mail-order publications, so they must be bringing in orders to the operators. Ads for a given mail-order product don't keep appearing unless they're producing enough orders to realize a good profit.

COPYRIGHT PROTECTION FOR YOUR MATERIAL

If you intend to offer any kind of informational booklet, pamphlet, correspondence course, or similar material by mail order, some general understanding of the copyright laws would be helpful.

When you create certain materials, you automatically acquire certain rights. The best way to understand a copyright is to think of it as a form of protection provided through the law of a country to authors of literary, artistic, musical, dramatic, or other intellectual works.

A separate or individual copyright must be obtained for each work, in order to have full protection.

Exclusive Rights in Copyrighted Works

The owner of the copyright has the exclusive rights:

1.   to reproduce the copyrighted work in copies or phonorecords;
2.   to prepare derivative works based upon the copyrighted work;
3.   to distribute copies or phonorecords of the copyrighted work to the public by sale or other transfer of ownership, or by rental, lease, or lending;
4.   in the case of literary, musical, dramatic, and choreographic works, pantomimes, and motion pictures and other audiovisual works, to perform the copyrighted work publicly; and
5.   in the case of literary, musical, dramatic, and choreographic works, pantomimes, and pictorial, graphic, or sculptural works, including the individual images of a motion picture or other audiovisual work, to display the copyrighted work publicly.

Subject matter of copyright: In general

The following types of material can be copyrighted. This is not a complete list, but it will give you a good idea of the range:

(a) Copyright protection subsists, in accordance with this title, in original works of authorship fixed in any tangible medium of expression, now known or later developed, from which they can be perceived, reproduced or otherwise communicated, either directly or with the aid of a machine or device. Works of authorship include the following categories:

1.   literary works; (see attached definition)
2.   musical works, including any accompanying words;
3.   dramatic works, including any accompanying music;
4.   pantomimes and choreographic works;
5.   pictorial, graphic, and sculptural works;
6.   motion pictures and other audiovisual works; and
7.   sound recordings.

(b) In no case does copyright protection for an original work of authorship extend to any idea, procedure, process system, method of operation, concept, principle, or discovery, regardless of the form in which it is described, explained, illustrated, or embodied in such work.

FORM TX
UNITED STATES COPYRIGHT OFFICE

REGISTRATION NUMBER

TX   TXU
EFFECTIVE DATE OF REGISTRATION

Month   Day   Year

DO NOT WRITE ABOVE THIS LINE. IF YOU NEED MORE SPACE, USE A SEPARATE CONTINUATION SHEET.

1

TITLE OF THIS WORK ▼

PREVIOUS OR ALTERNATIVE TITLES ▼

PUBLICATION AS A CONTRIBUTION   If this work was published as a contribution to a periodical, serial, or collection, give information about the collective work in which the contribution appeared.   **Title of Collective Work ▼**

If published in a periodical or serial give: Volume ▼   Number ▼   Issue Date ▼   On Pages ▼

2

a

NAME OF AUTHOR ▼   DATES OF BIRTH AND DEATH
                                                        Year Born ▼   Year Died ▼

Was this contribution to the work a "work made for hire"?   □ Yes   □ No   AUTHOR'S NATIONALITY OR DOMICILE   Name of Country   OR { Citizen of ▶ _____   Domiciled in ▶ _____   WAS THIS AUTHOR'S CONTRIBUTION TO THE WORK   Anonymous? □ Yes □ No   Pseudonymous? □ Yes □ No   If the answer to either of these questions is "Yes," see detailed instructions

NATURE OF AUTHORSHIP   Briefly describe nature of the material created by this author in which copyright is claimed. ▼

NOTE

Under the law, the "author" of a "work made for hire" is generally the employer, not the employee (see instructions). For any part of this work that was "made for hire" check "Yes" in the space provided, give the employer (or other person for whom the work was prepared) as "Author" of that part, and leave the space for dates of birth and death blank.

b

NAME OF AUTHOR ▼   DATES OF BIRTH AND DEATH
                                                        Year Born ▼   Year Died ▼

Was this contribution to the work a "work made for hire"?   □ Yes   □ No   AUTHOR'S NATIONALITY OR DOMICILE   Name of country   OR { Citizen of ▶ _____   Domiciled in ▶ _____   WAS THIS AUTHOR'S CONTRIBUTION TO THE WORK   Anonymous? □ Yes □ No   Pseudonymous? □ Yes □ No   If the answer to either of these questions is "Yes," see detailed instructions

NATURE OF AUTHORSHIP   Briefly describe nature of the material created by this author in which copyright is claimed. ▼

c

NAME OF AUTHOR ▼   DATES OF BIRTH AND DEATH
                                                        Year Born ▼   Year Died ▼

Was this contribution to the work a "work made for hire"?   □ Yes   □ No   AUTHOR'S NATIONALITY OR DOMICILE   Name of Country   OR { Citizen of ▶ _____   Domiciled in ▶ _____   WAS THIS AUTHOR'S CONTRIBUTION TO THE WORK   Anonymous? □ Yes □ No   Pseudonymous? □ Yes □ No   If the answer to either of these questions is "Yes," see detailed instructions

NATURE OF AUTHORSHIP   Briefly describe nature of the material created by this author in which copyright is claimed. ▼

3

YEAR IN WHICH CREATION OF THIS WORK WAS COMPLETED   This information must be given in all cases.   ◄ Year   DATE AND NATION OF FIRST PUBLICATION OF THIS PARTICULAR WORK   Complete this information ONLY if this work has been published.   Month ▶ _____ Day ▶ _____ Year ▶ _____   ◄ Nation

4

COPYRIGHT CLAIMANT(S)   Name and address must be given even if the claimant is the same as the author given in space 2.▼

APPLICATION RECEIVED

ONE DEPOSIT RECEIVED

TWO DEPOSITS RECEIVED

REMITTANCE NUMBER AND DATE

DO NOT WRITE HERE OFFICE USE ONLY

See instructions before completing this space

TRANSFER If the claimant(s) named here in space 4 are different from the author(s) named in space 2, give a brief statement of how the claimant(s) obtained ownership of the copyright.▼

MORE ON BACK ▶   • Complete all applicable spaces (numbers 5-11) on the reverse side of this page.   • See detailed instructions.   • Sign the form at line 10.   DO NOT WRITE HERE   Page 1 of _____ pages

Copyright Form

EXAMINED BY	FORM TX
CHECKED BY	

□ CORRESPONDENCE Yes	FOR COPYRIGHT OFFICE USE ONLY
□ DEPOSIT ACCOUNT FUNDS USED	

DO NOT WRITE ABOVE THIS LINE. IF YOU NEED MORE SPACE, USE A SEPARATE CONTINUATION SHEET.

PREVIOUS REGISTRATION Has registration for this work, or for an earlier version of this work, already been made in the Copyright Office?
□ Yes   □ No If your answer is "Yes," why is another registration being sought? (Check appropriate box) ▼
□ This is the first published edition of a work previously registered in unpublished form.
□ This is the first application submitted by this author as copyright claimant.
□ This is a changed version of the work, as shown by space 6 on this application.
If your answer is "Yes," give: **Previous Registration Number** ▼   **Year of Registration** ▼

5

DERIVATIVE WORK OR COMPILATION Complete both space 6a & 6b for a derivative work; complete only 6b for a compilation.
a. Preexisting Material Identify any preexisting work or works that this work is based on or incorporates. ▼

b. Material Added to This Work Give a brief, general statement of the material that has been added to this work and in which copyright is claimed. ▼

6

See instructions before completing this space.

MANUFACTURERS AND LOCATIONS If this is a published work consisting preponderantly of nondramatic literary material in English, the law may require that the copies be manufactured in the United States or Canada for full protection. If so, the names of the manufacturers who performed certain processes, and the places where these processes were performed **must be given**. See instructions for details.
Names of Manufacturers ▼   **Places of Manufacture** ▼

7

REPRODUCTION FOR USE OF BLIND OR PHYSICALLY HANDICAPPED INDIVIDUALS   A signature on this form at space 10, and a check in one of the boxes here in space 8, constitutes a non-exclusive grant of permission to the Library of Congress to reproduce and distribute solely for the blind and physically handicapped and under the conditions and limitations prescribed by the regulations of the Copyright Office: (1) copies of the work identified in space 1 of this application in Braille (or similar tactile symbols); or (2) phonorecords embodying a fixation of a reading of that work; or (3) both.
a □ Copies and Phonorecords   b □ Copies Only   c □ Phonorecords Only

8

See instructions

DEPOSIT ACCOUNT If the registration fee is to be charged to a Deposit Account established in the Copyright Office, give name and number of Account.
Name ▼   **Account Number** ▼

9

CORRESPONDENCE Give name and address to which correspondence about this application should be sent. Name/Address/Apt/City/State/Zip ▼

Area Code & Telephone Number ▶

Be sure to give your daytime phone ◀ number.

CERTIFICATION* I, the undersigned, hereby certify that I am the
Check one ▶
□ author
□ other copyright claimant
□ owner of exclusive right(s)
□ authorized agent of _____
     Name of author or other copyright claimant, or owner of exclusive right(s) ▲
of the work identified in this application and that the statements made by me in this application are correct to the best of my knowledge.

Typed or printed name and date ▼ If this is a published work, this date must be the same as or later than the date of publication given in space 3.
_____ date ▶ _____

☞ Handwritten signature (X) ▼

10

MAIL CERTIFICATE TO

Certificate will be mailed in window envelope

Name ▼

Number/Street/Apartment Number ▼

City/State/ZIP ▼

Have you:
• Completed all necessary spaces?
• Signed your application in space 10?
• Enclosed check or money order for $10 payable to *Register of Copyrights*?
• Enclosed your deposit material with the application and fee?
MAIL TO: Register of Copyrights, Library of Congress, Washington, D.C. 20559

11

* 17 U.S.C. § 508(e): Any person who knowingly makes a false representation of a material fact in the application for copyright registration provided for by section 409, or in any written statement filed in connection with the application, shall be fined not more than $2,500.

☆ U.S. GOVERNMENT PRINTING OFFICE: 1983: 381-278/507

Sept. 1983—600,000

Copyright Form (*contd.*)

Filling Out Application Form TX

Detach and read these instructions before completing this form. Make sure all applicable spaces have been filled in before you return this form.

BASIC INFORMATION

When to Use This Form: Use Form TX for registration of published or unpublished non-dramatic literary works, excluding periodicals or serial issues. This class includes a wide variety of works: fiction, non-fiction, poetry, textbooks, reference works, directories, catalogs, advertising copy, compilations of information, and computer programs. For periodicals and serials, use Form SE.

Deposit to Accompany Application: An application for copyright registration must be accompanied by a deposit consisting of copies or phonorecords representing the entire work for which registration is to be made. The following are the general deposit requirements as set forth in the statute:

Unpublished Work: Deposit one complete copy (or phonorecord).

Published Work: Deposit two complete copies (or phonorecords) of the best edition.

Work First Published Outside the United States: Deposit one complete copy (or phonorecord) of the first foreign edition.

Contribution to a Collective Work: Deposit one complete copy (or phonorecord) of the best edition of the collective work.

The Copyright Notice: For published works, the law provides that a copyright notice in a specified form "shall be placed on all publicly distributed copies from which the work can be visually perceived." Use of the copyright notice is the responsibility of the copyright owner and does not require advance permission from the Copyright Office. The required form of the notice for copies generally consists of three elements: (1) the symbol "©", or the word "Copyright," or the abbreviation "Copr."; (2) the year of first publication; and (3) the name of the owner of copyright. For example: "© 1981 Constance Porter." The notice is to be affixed to the copies "in such manner and location as to give reasonable notice of the claim of copyright."

For further information about copyright registration, notice, or special questions relating to copyright problems, write:

Information and Publications Section, LM-455
Copyright Office
Library of Congress
Washington, D.C. 20559

LINE-BY-LINE INSTRUCTIONS

1 SPACE 1: Title

Title of This Work: Every work submitted for copyright registration must be given a title to identify that particular work. If the copies or phonorecords of the work bear a title (or an identifying phrase that could serve as a title), transcribe that wording *completely* and *exactly* on the application. Indexing of the registration and future identification of the work will depend on the information you give here.

Previous or Alternative Titles: Complete this space if there are any additional titles for the work under which someone searching for the registration might be likely to look, or under which a document pertaining to the work might be recorded.

Publication as a Contribution: If the work being registered is a contribution to a periodical, serial, or collection, give the title of the contribution in the "Title of this Work" space. Then, in the line headed "Publication as a Contribution," give information about the collective work in which the contribution appeared.

2 SPACE 2: Author(s)

General Instructions: After reading these instructions, decide who are the "authors" of this work for copyright purposes. Then, unless the work is a "collective work," give the requested information about every "author" who contributed any appreciable amount of copyrightable matter to this version of the work. If you need further space, request additional Continuation sheets. In the case of a collective work, such as an anthology, collection of essays, or encyclopedia, give information about the author of the collective work as a whole.

Name of Author: The fullest form of the author's name should be given. Unless the work was "made for hire," the individual who actually created the work is its "author." In the case of a work made for hire, the statute provides that "the employer or other person for whom the work was prepared is considered the author."

What is a "Work Made for Hire"? A "work made for hire" is defined as: (1) "a work prepared by an employee within the scope of his or her employment"; or (2) "a work specially ordered or commissioned for use as a contribution to a collective work, as a part of a motion picture or other audiovisual work, as a translation, as a supplementary work, as a compilation, as an instructional text, as a test, as answer material for a test, or as an atlas, if the parties expressly agree in a written instrument signed by them that the work shall be considered a work made for hire." If you have checked "Yes" to indicate that the work was "made for hire," you must give the full legal name of the employer (or other person for whom the work was prepared). You may also include the name of the employee along with the name of the employer (for example: "Elster Publishing Co., employer for hire of John Ferguson").

"Anonymous" or "Pseudonymous" Work: An author's contribution to a work is "anonymous" if that author is not identified on the copies or phonorecords of the work. An author's contribution to a work is "pseudonymous" if that author is identified on the copies or phonorecords under a fictitious name. If the work is "anonymous" you may: (1) leave the line blank; or (2) state " anonymous" on the line; or (3) reveal the author's identity. If the work is "pseudonymous" you may : (1) leave the line blank; or (2) give the pseudonym and identify it as such (for example: "Huntley Haverstock, pseudonym"); or (3) reveal the author's name, making clear which is the real name and which is the pseudonym (for example: "Judith Barton, whose pseudonym is Madeline Elster"). However, the citizenship or domicile of the author **must** be given in all cases.

Dates of Birth and Death: If the author is dead, the statute requires that the year of death be included in the application unless the work is anonymous or pseudonymous. The author's birth date is optional, but is useful as a form of identification. Leave this space blank if the author's contribution was a "work made for hire."

Author's Nationality or Domicile: Give the country of which the author is a citizen, or the country in which the author is domiciled. Nationality or domicile **must** be given in all cases.

Nature of Authorship: After the words "Nature of Authorship" give a brief general statement of the nature of this particular author's contribution to the work. Examples: "Entire text"; "Coauthor of entire text"; "Chapters 11-14"; "Editorial revisions"; "Compilation and English translation"; "New text."

3 SPACE 3: Creation and Publication

General Instructions: Do not confuse "creation" with "publication." Every application for copyright registration must state "the year in which creation of the work was completed." Give the date and nation of first publication only if the work has been published.

Creation: Under the statute, a work is "created" when it is fixed in a copy or phonorecord for the first time. Where a work has been prepared over a period of time, the part of the work existing in fixed form on a particular date constitutes the created work on that date. The date you give here should be the year in which the author completed the particular version for which registration is now being sought, even if other versions exist or if further changes or additions are planned.

Publication: The statute defines "publication" as "the distribution of copies or phonorecords of a work to the public by sale or other transfer of ownership, or by rental, lease, or lending"; a work is also "published" if there has been an "offering to distribute copies or phonorecords to a group of persons for purposes of further distribution, public performance, or public display." Give the full date (month, day, year) when, and the country where, publication first occurred. If first publication took place simultaneously in the United States and other countries, it is sufficient to state "U.S.A."

4 SPACE 4: Claimant(s)

Name(s) and Address(es) of Copyright Claimant(s): Give the name(s) and address(es) of the copyright claimant(s) in this work even if the claimant is the same as the author. Copyright in a work belongs initially to the author of the work (including, in the case of a work made for hire, the employer or other person for whom the work was prepared). The copyright claimant is either the author of the work or a person or organization to whom the copyright initially belonging to the author has been transferred.

Transfer: The statute provides that, if the copyright claimant is not the author, the application for registration must contain "a brief statement of how the claimant obtained ownership of the copyright." If any copyright claimant named in space 4 is not an author named in space 2, give a brief, general statement summarizing the means by which that claimant obtained ownership of the copyright. Examples: "By written contract"; "Transfer of all rights by author"; "Assignment"; "By will." Do not attach transfer documents or other attachments or riders.

5 SPACE 5: Previous Registration

General Instructions: The questions in space 5 are intended to find out whether an earlier registration has been made for this work and, if so, whether there is any basis for a new registration. As a general rule, only one basic copyright registration can be made for the same version of a particular work.

Same Version: If this version is substantially the same as the work covered by a previous registration, a second registration is not generally possible unless: (1) the work has been registered in unpublished form and a second registration is now being sought to cover this first published edition; or (2) someone other than the author is identified as copyright claimant in the earlier registration, and the author is now seeking registration in his or her own name. If either of these two exceptions apply, check the appropriate box and give the earlier registration number and date. Otherwise, do not submit Form TX; instead, write the Copyright Office for information about supplementary registration or recordation of transfers of copyright ownership.

Changed Version: If the work has been changed, and you are now seeking registration to cover the additions or revisions, check the last box in space 5, give the earlier registration number and date, and complete both parts of space 6 in accordance with the instructions below.

Previous Registration Number and Date: If more than one previous registration has been made for the work, give the number and date of the latest registration.

6 SPACE 6: Derivative Work or Compilation

General Instructions: Complete space 6 if this work is a "changed version," "compilation," or "derivative work," and if it incorporates one or more earlier works that have already been published or registered for copyright, or that have fallen into the public domain. A "compilation" is defined as "a work formed by the collection and assembling of preexisting materials or of data that are selected, coordinated, or arranged in such a way that the resulting work as a whole constitutes an original work of authorship." A "derivative work" is "a work based on one or more preexisting works." Examples of derivative works include translations, fictionalizations, abridgments, condensations, or "any other form in which a work may be recast, transformed, or adapted." Derivative works also include works "consisting of editorial revisions, annotations, or other modifications" if these changes, as a whole, represent an original work of authorship.

Preexisting Material (space 6a): For derivative works, complete this space and space 6b. In space 6a identify the preexisting work that has been recast, transformed, or adapted. An example of preexisting material might be: "Russian version of Goncharov's 'Oblomov'." Do not complete space 6a for compilations.

Material Added to This Work (space 6b): Give a brief, general statement of the new material covered by the copyright claim for which registration is sought. **Derivative work** examples include: "Foreword, editing, critical annotations"; "Translation"; "Chapters 11-17." If the work is a **compilation**, describe both the compilation itself and the material that has been compiled. Example: "Compilation of certain 1917 Speeches by Woodrow Wilson." A work may be both a derivative work and compilation, in which case a sample statement might be: "Compilation and additional new material."

7 SPACE 7: Manufacturing Provisions

General Instructions. The copyright statute currently provides, as a general rule, that the copies of a published work "consisting preponderantly of nondramatic literary material in the English language" be manufactured in the United States or Canada in order to be lawfully imported and publicly distributed in the United States. If the work being registered is unpublished or not in English, leave this space blank. Complete this space if registration is sought for a published work "consisting preponderantly of nondramatic literary material that is in the English language." Identify those who manufactured the copies and where those manufacturing processes were performed. As an exception to the manufacturing provisions, the statute prescribes that, where manufacture has taken place outside the United States or Canada, a maximum of 2000 copies of the foreign edition may be imported into the United States without affecting the copyright owners' rights. For this purpose, the Copyright Office will issue an Import Statement upon request and payment of a fee of $3 at the time of registration or at any later time. For further information about import statements, write for Form IS.

8 SPACE 8: Reproduction for Use of Blind or Physically Handicapped Individuals

General Instructions: One of the major programs of the Library of Congress is to provide Braille editions and special recordings of works for the exclusive use of the blind and physically handicapped. In an effort to simplify and speed up the copyright licensing procedures that are a necessary part of this program, section 710 of the copyright statute provides for the establishment of a voluntary licensing system to be tied in with copyright registration. Copyright Office regulations provide that you may grant a license for such reproduction and distribution solely for the use of persons who are certified by competent authority as unable to read normal printed material as a result of physical limitations. The license is entirely voluntary, nonexclusive, and may be terminated upon 90 days notice.

How to Grant the License: If you wish to grant it, check one of the three boxes in space 8. Your check in one of these boxes, together with your signature in space 10, will mean that the Library of Congress can proceed to reproduce and distribute under the license without further paperwork. For further information, write for Circular R63.

9,10,11 SPACE 9, 10, 11: Fee, Correspondence, Certification, Return Address

Deposit Account: If you maintain a Deposit Account in the Copyright Office, identify it in space 9. Otherwise leave the space blank and send the fee of $10 with your application and deposit.

Correspondence (space 9): This space should contain the name, address, area code, and telephone number of the person to be consulted if correspondence about this application becomes necessary.

Certification (space 10): The application can not be accepted unless it bears the date and the **handwritten signature** of the author or other copyright claimant, or of the owner of exclusive right(s), or of the duly authorized agent of author, claimant, or owner of exclusive right(s).

Address for Return of Certificate (space 11): The address box must be completed legibly since the certificate will be returned in a window envelope.

Copyright Form (*contd.*)

FORM VA
UNITED STATES COPYRIGHT OFFICE

REGISTRATION NUMBER

VA   VAU

EFFECTIVE DATE OF REGISTRATION

Month   Day   Year

DO NOT WRITE ABOVE THIS LINE. IF YOU NEED MORE SPACE, USE A SEPARATE CONTINUATION SHEET.

1

TITLE OF THIS WORK ▼   NATURE OF THIS WORK ▼ See instructions

PREVIOUS OR ALTERNATIVE TITLES ▼

PUBLICATION AS A CONTRIBUTION   If this work was published as a contribution to a periodical, serial, or collection, give information about the collective work in which the contribution appeared.   Title of Collective Work ▼

If published in a periodical or serial give: Volume ▼   Number ▼   Issue Date ▼   On Pages ▼

2

a   NAME OF AUTHOR ▼   DATES OF BIRTH AND DEATH
                                                            Year Born ▼   Year Died ▼

Was this contribution to the work a   AUTHOR'S NATIONALITY OR DOMICILE   WAS THIS AUTHOR'S CONTRIBUTION TO
"work made for hire"?   Name of Country   THE WORK   If the answer to either
☐ Yes   OR { Citizen of ▶   Anonymous?   ☐ Yes ☐ No   of these questions is
☐ No   Domiciled in ▶   Pseudonymous? ☐ Yes ☐ No   "Yes." see detailed
                                                                                         instructions

NATURE OF AUTHORSHIP   Briefly describe nature of the material created by this author in which copyright is claimed. ▼

NOTE
Under the law,
the "author" of a
"work made for
hire" is generally
the employer,
not the em-
ployee (see in-
structions). For
any part of this
work that was
"made for hire"
check "Yes" in
the space pro-
vided, give the
employer (or
other person for
whom the work
was prepared)
as "Author" of
that part, and
leave the space
for dates of birth
and death blank.

b   NAME OF AUTHOR ▼   DATES OF BIRTH AND DEATH
                                                            Year Born ▼   Year Died ▼

Was this contribution to the work a   AUTHOR'S NATIONALITY OR DOMICILE   WAS THIS AUTHOR'S CONTRIBUTION TO
"work made for hire"?   Name of country   THE WORK   If the answer to either
☐ Yes   OR { Citizen of ▶   Anonymous?   ☐ Yes ☐ No   of these questions is
☐ No   Domiciled in ▶   Pseudonymous? ☐ Yes ☐ No   "Yes." see detailed
                                                                                         instructions.

NATURE OF AUTHORSHIP   Briefly describe nature of the material created by this author in which copyright is claimed. ▼

c   NAME OF AUTHOR ▼   DATES OF BIRTH AND DEATH
                                                            Year Born ▼   Year Died ▼

Was this contribution to the work a   AUTHOR'S NATIONALITY OR DOMICILE   WAS THIS AUTHOR'S CONTRIBUTION TO
"work made for hire"?   Name of Country   THE WORK   If the answer to either
☐ Yes   OR { Citizen of ▶   Anonymous?   ☐ Yes ☐ No   of these questions is
☐ No   Domiciled in ▶   Pseudonymous? ☐ Yes ☐ No   "Yes." see detailed
                                                                                         instructions

NATURE OF AUTHORSHIP   Briefly describe nature of the material created by this author in which copyright is claimed. ▼

3

YEAR IN WHICH CREATION OF THIS   DATE AND NATION OF FIRST PUBLICATION OF THIS PARTICULAR WORK
WORK WAS COMPLETED   This information   Complete this information   Month ▶   Day ▶   Year ▶
                     must be given   ONLY if this work
              ◀ Year in all cases.   has been published.   ◀ Nation

4

COPYRIGHT CLAIMANT(S) Name and address must be given even if the claimant is the   APPLICATION RECEIVED
same as the author given in space 2.▼

See instructions   ONE DEPOSIT RECEIVED
before completing
this space.   TWO DEPOSITS RECEIVED

TRANSFER If the claimant(s) named here in space 4 are different from the author(s) named   REMITTANCE NUMBER AND DATE
in space 2, give a brief statement of how the claimant(s) obtained ownership of the copyright.▼

DO NOT WRITE HERE OFFICE USE ONLY

MORE ON BACK ▶   • Complete all applicable spaces (numbers 5-9) on the reverse side of this page   DO NOT WRITE HERE
                 • See detailed instructions   • Sign the form at line 8   Page 1 of _____ pages

Copyright Form VA, for works of the visual arts

EXAMINED BY

CHECKED BY

☐ CORRESPONDENCE
Yes

☐ DEPOSIT ACCOUNT
FUNDS USED

FORM VA

FOR
COPYRIGHT
OFFICE
USE
ONLY

DO NOT WRITE ABOVE THIS LINE. IF YOU NEED MORE SPACE, USE A SEPARATE CONTINUATION SHEET.

PREVIOUS REGISTRATION Has registration for this work, or for an earlier version of this work, already been made in the Copyright Office?
☐ Yes ☐ No If your answer is "Yes," why is another registration being sought? (Check appropriate box) ▼
☐ This is the first published edition of a work previously registered in unpublished form.
☐ This is the first application submitted by this author as copyright claimant.
☐ This is a changed version of the work, as shown by space 6 on this application.
If your answer is "Yes," give: **Previous Registration Number** ▼   **Year of Registration** ▼

5

DERIVATIVE WORK OR COMPILATION Complete both space 6a & 6b for a derivative work; complete only 6b for a compilation.
a. **Preexisting Material** Identify any preexisting work or works that this work is based on or incorporates. ▼

b. **Material Added to This Work** Give a brief, general statement of the material that has been added to this work and in which copyright is claimed. ▼

6

See instructions
before completing
this space

DEPOSIT ACCOUNT If the registration fee is to be charged to a Deposit Account established in the Copyright Office, give name and number of Account.
Name ▼   **Account Number** ▼

7

CORRESPONDENCE Give name and address to which correspondence about this application should be sent. Name/Address/Apt/City/State/Zip ▼

Area Code & Telephone Number ▶

Be sure to
give your
daytime phone
◀ number

CERTIFICATION* I, the undersigned, hereby certify that I am the
Check only one ▼
☐ author
☐ other copyright claimant
☐ owner of exclusive right(s)
☐ authorized agent of
Name of author or other copyright claimant, or owner of exclusive right(s) ▲

8

of the work identified in this application and that the statements made
by me in this application are correct to the best of my knowledge.

Typed or printed name and date ▼ If this is a published work, this date must be the same as or later than the date of publication given in space 3.

date ▶

Handwritten signature (X) ▼

**MAIL
CERTIFI-
CATE TO**

Name ▼

Number/Street/Apartment Number ▼

City/State/ZIP ▼

Certificate
will be
mailed in
window
envelope

Have you:
• Completed all necessary spaces?
• Signed your application in space 8?
• Enclosed check or money order for $10 payable to Register of Copyrights?
• Enclosed your deposit material with the application and fee?
MAIL TO: Register of Copyrights, Library of Congress, Washington, D.C. 20559.

9

☆ U.S. GOVERNMENT PRINTING OFFICE: 1982: 361-278/53

July 1982-120,000

Form VA (contd.)

What Cannot Be Copyrighted

1.   Titles.

2.   Short phrases, names, slogans, and familiar symbols or designs.

3.   Plans, ideas, methods, devices, or systems.

4.   Blank forms used as time cards, diaries, bank checks, address books, report forms, and account books.

5.   Information that is not of original authorship—common knowledge—for example, sports event schedules, height-weight charts, and tape measures.

The Copyright Notice

Once copies have been produced and a work has been published, a copyright notice must appear on each copy. The notice consists of three required elements:

1.   The name of the copyright owner or owners

2.   The year the work was published

3.   The word "Copyright," its abbreviation "Copr.," or the symbol ©

Here is an example of the correct use of this required notice:

© Bill Brown 1985

For a book or material published in book form, the notice should go on the title page or on the page following it, i.e., the reverse side of the title page.

Unpublished works do not have to include the notice, according to law. But it would be wise to have it on any copies, so the work can't be mistakenly published without notice.

New Changes in the Copyright Law

In January, 1978, a Copyright Revision Bill replaced the old law. Here are some of the new law's changes:

1.   Copyright protection of a work lasts for the author's lifetime plus 50 years. This applies to any work created after January 1, 1978. Works already copyrighted before 1978 can now be

renewed for an additional 47 years, rather than the period of 28 years specified in the old law.

2.   The new law has raised the royalty on music recordings from 2¢ to 2-¾¢ or ½¢ per minute of playing time, whichever amount is larger.

3.   The operators of jukeboxes must now pay royalties for music used.

4.   Published or unpublished works are now covered by the US copyright law.

A full copy of the new law may be obtained from the Copyright Office in Washington, D.C.. Highlights and summary information on various aspects of the new changes are also available in circulars R99 and R15a from the same office.

Steps in Securing a Copyright

1.   Write the Register of Copyrights at the following address:

> Register of Copyrights
> Library of Congress
> Washington, D.C. 20559

2.   Request the application form for the type of work you wish to copyright.

3.   Complete the application form for whatever you wish to register.

4.   Enclose the correct fee with your application. Currently the fee is $10.00 for published or unpublished works. If in doubt as to the fee, simply write to the Copyright Office and request fee information concerning the type of work you wish to copyright.

5.   Mail your application fee and one copy of the work (if unpublished) or two copies (if published) to the Register of Copyrights. Be sure to mail the application, fee, and copies in the same package.

6.   Your certificate of copyright will be mailed to you in several weeks. Keep in a safe place.

CONSIDER BOOKSELLING BY MAIL

You might want to think about selling full length books by mail. There are a number of book companies that sell by mail. You simply write to them on your company letterhead and state that you want to sell their books as a dealer. Some book companies may require previous experience in selling books, but many of them will be glad to drop-ship the orders you send them. This means that all you do is send the company the book orders you receive, and the book company will fill the orders for you under your company name. You are usually required to supply the shipping labels.

I did this myself in a small way for about a year, acting as a dealer for a company in Kansas. For $5.00 the book company sent me 1,000 advertising flyers that were, in effect, order forms. My company name and address was imprinted on the flyers. Each flyer listed the categories of books available to a buyer. On the reverse side was space for the buyer's name and address.

This book company featured a bargain offer of forty books for only $3.00. The books, however, were very small in size. But consider the appeal of their offer. For $3.00 a buyer could get as many as forty little books on the subject categories of his or her choice. No wonder this particular little book company has been doing business for years.

I sold a lot of those little books to buyers all over the country. I got orders in two ways. I ran small classified ads in different mail-order magazines, and I also sent the subject category flyers by direct mail to known mail-order buyers. Even after I developed and produced my first exclusive product, I kept sending out those advertising flyers. Whenever I filled an order for my own exclusive product, I would include a few flyers with the package. I sold a lot of those little books. My usual profit on each order was $1.50. That's not much, but it added up as the orders kept coming in each month. Being new to mail order, it was good to have a steady cash flow to build my confidence and enthusiasm. I was actually doing business.

At this writing, this little book company is still in business. You might want to contact them about becoming a dealer for them. It would be starting in a small way, of course, but to actually receive money-laden mail orders for this relatively trouble-free drop-ship arrangement will increase your interest and enthusiasm and certainly build your confidence. Here is the name and address of the company:

Little Blue Book Company
Girard, Kansas 66743

Maybe you would prefer to sell full size and full length books by mail. That's fine too. You can get the names of book companies wanting dealers in mail-order magazines like *Specialty Salesman* and *Salesman's Opportunity*. Ads for book dealers appear regularly in most issues. You can write to the companies for the details of their dealership arrangements and compare your profits under various companies. Reading some of the mail-order publications regularly will supply you with the names of many book companies that would be glad to have you work with them as a dealer. A special advantage of selling books is that they appeal to all ages. The potential market is enormous.

SELLING A SERVICE

If you prefer to sell a service, do some thinking about how you might help people in some way. Perhaps you have some special type of knowledge that you could use in a mail-order service. Search your background. Almost every person is good at something or has special knowledge about one subject or another. Think about your hobbies, interests, and talents. You might find several possibilities for services you could offer by mail. This might be the best approach for you in mail order. For example, people who are experienced in advertising have used their ability to start an advertising service. I've done this myself and now serve a number of national clients as an advertising consultant. This is in addition to the products I sell by mail order.

A WARNING

Whatever product you come up with, don't overstock the item at first. Wait until you've had a chance to test your product out with ads in key mail-order publications. Once you have an item that is pulling in orders consistently and allows you a healthy profit after your expense in producing, stocking, and shipping it to buyers, you can then stock all you need of the item to fill incoming orders. Many newcomers to mail order have fallen into the trap of overstocking their product only to find out later that not enough orders have come in to deplete the stock on hand. Test first for an initial response to your ad, and when your product looks like a winner, you can then increase your stock accordingly.

YOU CAN SELL SOMEONE ELSE'S PRODUCT

If you prefer not to originate a product yourself, you can still get into mail order by selling an existing product. There are numerous product suppliers that will drop-ship their items to your mail-order customers. In order to use this method, you must send your customer's order (with the name and address of the buyer typed on a label that has your company name on it) to the supplier. You get orders by running your own ads or sales letters.

The names and addresses of various product suppliers can be found in mail-order magazines, classified telephone directories, statewide industrial directories, and other special directories found in most public libraries.

KNOW THE MARKET FOR YOUR PRODUCT

Whatever the product, service, or offer you start off with, do some careful thinking about the market for it. Try to determine who your prospects are and their approximate age. If you're trying to reach teenagers and young people, for example, certain publications would be better than others. If senior citizens are your main target, special publications for older people would be best suited for your ads.

Take plenty of time deciding what your first product or offer will be. It's a vital decision. Choosing the right product to sell is considered the most important requirement for success in mail order.

Soon after World War II, one man hit upon the idea of selling cuckoo clocks. He imported them from a manufacturer he met while serving in the army in Germany. The manufacturer had been a friend of his during his stay in Germany, and so the two men arranged to work together.

These cuckoo clocks were the first product choice of Brainerd Mellinger. The clocks sold well by mail. Today Mellinger is an internationally known trader and businessman. He says that he owes every penny of his fortune to mail order.

THINKING AHEAD

Thinking ahead can make a lot of difference in your business. After you make a choice of a first product, you will need to line up a reliable source of supply for your product, unless you plan to produce it yourself. Then you must plan your ads and determine the best times to run them. Much advance thinking and planning are called for in mail order. Thinking ahead is really a small price to pay for substantial and lasting success.

DROP-SHIP ARRANGEMENTS

You might prefer to sell an existing product, rather than produce your own. If so, then the key word to keep in mind is "drop-ship." A drop-ship is an arrangement in which manufacturers offer their products to you at a special discount price and ship the items directly to your customers. All that you're usually required to supply are the payment for the order and a completed shipping label. A company that agrees to work with you will explain any other necessary requirements.

It is important to communicate with any manufacturer you contact in a professional way. If you write to leading manufacturers in longhand and without using a letterhead, they probably won't reply. They want to deal only with serious-minded individuals who conduct their business in a professional manner. So be sure to type all letters to manufacturers on your letterhead.

The profit potential of drop-ship arrangements is good. If you can buy an item from a manufacturer for three of four dollars and then sell it to your customers for eight or nine dollars, your profits will add up. In most cases, the profit margin is very high. In other words, many manufacturers will offer a larger discount than you'd usually receive from a wholesaler, allowing you a higher profit margin.

Setting Up a Drop-Ship Agreement

There are many manufacturers of a variety of products that are willing to drop-ship for mail-order companies. Here are some proven tips to help you set up a drop-ship agreement with a manufacturer.

1. Look through trade journals and directories for the names of leading manufacturers. The Yellow Pages also list many manufacturers.

2. Write to manufacturers on your business letterhead. Your letters should be typed. Keep carbon copies of all letters sent to manufacturers.

3. State your willingness to pay for your first product purchases in advance, when writing to manufacturers. Perhaps you can establish credit a bit later, after you've made several orders.

4. Try to be as businesslike as possible. If you're writing to request details about a particular product, enclose a self-addressed, stamped envelope (one of your business envelopes).

5. Explain in your letter to a manufacturer that you wish to offer your mail-order customers new products of value, and that you believe that their company has such a product. Ask for descriptive material on the products you like and what the discount price will be to you as a mail-order dealer. Close your letter with a request for an early reply.

Special Sources for Drop-Ship Selling

By using some special sources found in most large libraries, you can find a number of good drop-ship manufacturers to contact. Two of the best sources for manufacturers are *McCrae's Blue Book* and *Thomas's Register of American Manufacturers*. Both are large and accurate directories listing the name, address, and specific products of all leading United States manufacturers. Other countries have similar directories or trade journals in which key manufacturers are listed.

A STRONG REASON TO BE ENTHUSED ABOUT MAIL ORDER

According to the Census Bureau there will be a whopping 300 million people in the United States alone by the year 2000. This will reflect an increase of 87 million or more between today and the end of the century. The population in most other countries all over the world is also growing. This means a huge and ever-growing number of customers to buy your mail-order products and services. I've done well, myself, with self-improvement products. So keep the golden potential of self-help books, products, and services in mind. Find or develop a product or service you can start with. Begin planning now to get your slice of this billion dollar mail-order pie.

Some Product Ideas to Get You Started

A study of the mail-order industry shows that a great many people enter the business with either a booklet like we've described or with a specialty or novelty item. Quite a few of these mail-order operations are doing a healthy business today selling the same basic product that they started with. Some of the following items are now being offered; others are new ideas that might work well for you. Some are more suitable for mail order than others. All of them will stimulate your thinking about products.

Old Records. Buy old LP (long playing) records and sell them to music lovers for a profit. Many record buyers don't wish to pay the high prices of today's records.

Elvis Presley Materials. These could include written tributes to the late singer, a short booklet of poems composed by you about Elvis, facts about his life collected and printed in a special momento-style form, or even a recorded tape message about Elvis. Even Elvis toothbrushes are being sold at this writing. In some cases, however, special permission might have to be obtained to sell Elvis-related items.

Another idea for an Elvis-related offer is a correspondence course about the great entertainer. It would take some time to develop, but it might be tremendously profitable. You would have to decide how many parts to include in your course and the length of each. Millions of Elvis fans all over the world might respond warmly to a well-done course about the life of the king of rock and roll. Proof of this demand for an Elvis course is an actual course currently being conducted on Elvis at the University of Tennessee at Knoxville. The course is slated to become a part of the regular curriculum of the university. Students will earn regular college credits for this special Elvis course, which was planned even before his death.

Conservation Kits.   These could include a checklist or pamphlet of 50 or more ways to save energy and conserve on cooling, heating, and refrigeration. Millions are very interested in such information, so your sales should be very good.

Do-It-Yourself Divorce Kits.   This item has been sold successfully in some states. With the skyrocketing divorce rate, there's no doubt that a huge market is still out there for such an item. You could tailor your divorce kit to the divorce laws of your country or home state.

A former barber in Rochester, New York hit on a clever new way to make money. Not long ago, he was selling do-it-yourself divorce kits for $75 each and "separation" kits for $25. The kits included all the required forms and information on the procedures necessary to obtain a divorce or separation in the state of New York.

If sold in other states, each kit would, of course, have to provide the correct forms for that particular location. By meeting the requirements of each state, the kits could probably be sold everywhere.

Over a million divorces are obtained each year in the United States alone, so demand for the kits should be quite strong. The fact that many lawyers charge $700 or more for a divorce strengthens the demand even more. Certain age groups seem to have a higher divorce rate than others. For the group under 34, the divorce rate is presently double what it was only 10 years ago. This group might be a good target for your ads.

Guidance Services for Retired People.   Millions of retired people have little or no idea of where to retire. You could do some research on a list of communities or retirement villages in your area, rating them on the basis of such factors as quality and relative cost.

There are other ways to help retired people. Vacation guides, health protection tips, and information on Social Security benefits are a few items of interest to the retirement set. Material on interesting things for retired people to do could also be produced and offered. A lot of retired persons don't know what to do with all their time.

Special Information Booklets for Teenagers. A strong possible title might be "What Every Teenager Should Know." The information could cover all kinds of useful facts that would be helpful to teens. Mailing-list brokers can provide you with a huge number of teenage prospects (see chapter 9). The latest estimates indicate that teenagers spent an enormous $28.7 billion last year on all types of products.

Guides to the National Parks. Camping has become big business. Millions everywhere hit the trail for the great outdoors every season. Why not offer them a special guide to the national parks and key camping areas of your country? This product could be a year-round mail-order seller because families and camping enthusiasts are always thinking about their next trip.

Special Newsletters for Selected Markets. These might vary from just two pages to ten or more. The idea is to decide on the market that you want to reach in advance. Who would be the best or most likely prospects for a newsletter? Families might buy a newsletter if the material in it helped or informed them. Child guidance tips might sell and be very welcome. One possibility might be to tell families how they can keep from worrying about their children.

Fortunes have been made from popular newsletters. Years ago, one enterprising man launched a 14-page weekly newsletter. He promoted it and watched it grow to more than 8,000 copies a week. Today, this former newsletter has become a newspaper and is the largest conservative organ in the United States. The publication, known as *Human Events*, has a current weekly circulation over 80,000.

Special Lists. One of the top best-selling books of recent years was *The Book of Lists*. Directories have sold well for many years. Why not think about compiling lists of prospects, unusual companies, or anything else that others might find useful? Then offer the lists by mail for a fair price.

Booklets on Reincarnation, Astrology, or Some Aspect of the Occult. People never seem to tire of reading and speculating about the world of the occult. Dr. Raymond Moody's book on immortality survival, *Life After Life*, has sold in the millions. The occult offers all kinds of product and service possibilities.

Sports Equipment Items. You might be able to come up with some accessories connected with this product area. Consider this idea carefully. Ask yourself what could help tennis players, boat owners or joggers.

Tests. Many people everywhere are curious by nature. All kinds of tests (forms to be filled in or questions to be answered) are therefore worth considering. People enjoy answering test questions and adding up their scores. You could easily come up with a winner here. A number of tests are now being sold, but there's certainly room for more. The cost of having test forms printed is low, so the profit margin is good.

Clothes Accessories. A study done by the research department of *Seventeen* magazine on apparel spending by teenage American girls revealed that the total estimated annual amount spent on *all* apparel is $15,821,000.000. Teen girls spent $13.2 billion for their spring wardrobe in 1984, including $1,478,802,000 for accessories, and $8,726,628,000 for outerwear (coats, suits, jackets, dresses, skirts, pants, blouses, sweaters, and tops).

Recorded Sounds. Amazing as it may seem, there are now records of whale and bird sounds. And they sell.

Tape Cassette Messages. Perhaps you can tell others how to do something. If so, you might sell tape recorded messages for $6 to $10 each. Plan for about 120 spoken words a minute when recording.

Speed Reading Courses. These could be done in the form of a booklet, record, or tape. People everywhere are reading more than ever. A great many readers would like to be able to read much faster while maintaining good comprehension.

Don't forget one thing about courses in general. Many people are very responsive to self-improvement courses. Show them how your course can help them, and you're going to make a lot of sales. Many individuals dislike the work they do for a living. Millions of workers around the globe are looking for a better and more profitable future.

Convince them that your product or service can help them to get ahead and you'll make money.

Loneliness Market Items.   This market alone could make you rich. Loneliness is destroying a lot of people these days.

The Census Bureau reports that since the early 1970s there's been a 43 percent increase in the number of people who live alone. Most of those who live alone in the United States are women—especially those who are 65 and over.

Loneliness can affect anyone. Even film stars, entertainers, and celebrities are lonely sometimes. The case of Marilyn Monroe is a tragic example. She was often lonely in the last years before her death. Actress Inger Stevens, who took her own life, told a friend not long before that "I get so lonely I could scream." Could you offer a product or service that would help lonely people? Maybe you could come up with something to prevent loneliness or help people to cope with it. You might do the world a great service and get rich besides.

Inflation Fighters.   Prospects will pay well for items that show them how to handle inflation and get more for their money.

One man in California actually figured out a way to live fairly well on as little as $4,000 a year. He buys everything at bargain prices and doesn't drive a car at all, but he claims his system works. Not long ago, this man said that he had never been happier, saying, "I've left the rat race for good."

Maybe you can work up an effective inflation-fighting system and sell it by mail at a handsome profit. Jimmy Carter summed up the problem of the rising cost of living most accurately when he said that "inflation has hit us hard not in the luxuries but in the essentials of life like food and heat." Any problem as universal as inflation creates an enormous market for solutions.

Do-It-Yourself Auto Repair Guides.   Your offer could range from a handy guide sheet to a full-length manual. This is a recession-proof item. It could sell for you all year long.

Things to Sell at Flea Markets.   Why not compile a list of popular flea markets and items that could be sold at them. There should be a market for such a source list, and it wouldn't take you long to start selling it.

Handwriting Analysis Services.   There are reports of people earning handsome profits from this type of service. Customers mail you a sample of their writing for an analysis.

Mind Control Products and Systems. This idea covers manuals, guide sheets, records, tapes, booklets, test forms, and complete correspondence courses.

Menu Services. Plan menus for six months or a year and sell them by mail. One woman is reported to be earning over $75,000 a year doing menus.

Guides on How to Winterize Pets. Dogs, cats, and other pets feel the bitter cold of winter too. You might consider producing a manual or simple pamphlet telling pet owners how to keep their dogs and cats warm until another spring rolls around.

Literary Agencies. Sell the articles, stories, newspaper features, and books of aspiring writers to international magazines, newspapers, syndicates, and book publishers. A 10 percent commission rate is standard, but some agents also charge a reading fee for their service.

MAIL-ORDER PRODUCTS THAT HAVE SOLD WELL

Many of the products listed and discussed below are being sold successfully today. It is helpful to know what specific products have chalked up a good sales performance. You might want to sell something similar to these proven order pullers. Here they are:

Home Study Courses on Writing Short Paragraphs for Money. This product has been selling well for many years. Orders are obtained mostly from classified ads. Those who see the ads write in for free details on the course. Follow-up sales literature is then sent. The appeal here is strong, and most of those who respond to the ads believe that writing short paragraphs for money is an entirely possible and realistic venture. It's no wonder that this product has been a highly successful and profitable one for years.

Records that Teach Self-hypnosis. Here is another good seller by mail. When the owner of this product first advertised, he was flooded with orders and made a large profit. This record is still selling, evidently, because the ad is continually seen in many leading mail-order publications.

Gadgets and Instructional Materials to Help a Person Play the Guitar. These products range from simple instructional booklets to full-length courses and devices, all of which can help one learn the basic chords on the guitar. There are products and booklets for both beginners and experienced guitarists. Prices range from $3.98 on up.

Products for Pets. Don't forget that many pets are treated better than human beings. I have actually heard of a woman who feeds her cocker spaniel bacon and raisin toast every morning. Pet-oriented products are here to stay, since millions of people will probably always have pets and buy all kinds of things for them. Just a few of these pet items include doghouses, dog collars, dog and cat play toys, pet certificates, and pet clothing items.

Magnifying Eyeglasses. This simple product has been a good seller for years. Many people today are living longer and there's a steady, ever-growing market for this kind of item. Magnifying eyeglasses are sold year-round for personal use or as a gift item. Products that only sell well at certain times—such as at Christmas—are naturally limited. Try to pick a product that will sell at any time of year.

Correspondence Courses. Study courses by mail offer tangible benefits to the buyer in the form of a happier life, a higher income, and a more fulfilling job. Many courses are published exclusively by one company and can only be taken by mail order. Correspondence courses in advertising, hotel and motel management, real estate, music, aviation, modeling and fashion, and many others are being sold successfully through the mail today.

Mailbox Covers. This item has been consistently advertised in the mail-order shopping pages of *House Beautiful* magazine for many years. The major appeal of mailbox covers is their immediate usefulness to the buyer.

Hobbies. Many profitable mail-order companies have been built around hobbies. Coin and stamp collecting are two good examples. One mail-order businessman does well by offering a stamp investment counseling service. Stamps and coins have been offered through mail order for several decades. Mail-order companies also sell autographs and letters of famous people, matchbooks, postcards, war souvenirs, and other collectibles. So give some thought to possible product-hobby tie-ins.

Bar Lamps and Accessories. Some mail-order firms specialize in this type of merchandise. Bar accessories are usually sold by direct mail, but bar lamps are sometimes sold by display ads. Some companies have sold hundreds of thousands of dollars worth of these bar items.

Boots for Outdoorsmen. The L.L. Bean Company, the largest mail-order firm in New England, began its business in 1912 with this product. The boots are of an original design and sold exclusively by mail. The grandson of the original owner runs the company today and has increased the business 6 percent a year with gross sales of $237.4 million in 1983. The L.L. Bean Company catalog also offering colonial furniture, general store products, and equipment for skiing, is mailed to an estimated 60 million people. A catalog is a worthy goal to strive for, but it takes time, experience, and a growing line of proven sellers to develop a good catalog. A catalog that will consistently produce orders can be a virtual gold mine.

Colonial Style Bookracks and Pipe Stands. These products are sold successfully by a well-known mail-order company called Yield House. An interesting point to remember is that many mail-order firms in New England began their businesses with products that had a definite tie-in with that section of the country. Maybe you can think of a product or service that would have special appeal to potential customers in the area where you now live. Keep it in mind. It could result in a new and profitable product for you.

Novelty Items. Products in this category are different from what can be found in stores today. Jokes, magic tricks, and handmade and imported products are good examples. Remember the hula hoop? When it hit the market its novelty appeal was enormous. There was nothing else like it and it sold in the millions. One of the best bits of advice to guide you in your mail-order business is this: Try to develop a product that will have mass appeal. Any item that satisfies the ambitions, basic desires, and needs of many people is a good choice for your first mail-order product.

Boutique Items. By inscribing words, names, phrases, figures, and cartoon characters on napkins, handkerchiefs, savings banks, wallets, gloves, shirts, jackets, towels, and similar items, they can be turned into something special and unusual. Ask yourself what might be added to an existing product to give it a new effect and appeal. I keep repeating this idea because it's so important. With a little imagination, even an ordinary item like a napkin can be turned into a fine product. This adding-something-new-to-make-it-more-unusual idea can open up many new product possibilities for you.

Art Supplies. As long as there are people interested in sketching, drawing, painting, and artwork in general, art supplies will continue to sell. Buying by mail is an easy and inexpensive way to obtain art supplies.

Toys and Games. These have sold steadily since the early days of mail order. Toys and games sell best during the Christmas season, but with effective ads and sales literature they can be sold throughout the year. Maybe you could dream up a new game, but until you've gained more experience in mail order it is usually safer to offer a tried and tested one.

Religious Items. These include candles, cards, Bibles, bookmarks, framed prayers and religious sayings, and pictures of Bible characters. To get an idea of what is available, visit several of the larger Christian bookstores, which usually sell a variety of religious items. Also, look over the ads offering religious items in mail-order publications.

Gifts. These continue to be consistent sellers in mail order. There are mail-order companies that have developed complete catalogs of gift items. These catalogs are advertised by direct mail and sometimes by classified and display ads. The increasing number of gift stores is one clear sign of the profitability of mail-order gift items. In addition to acquiring stock through mail order, many gift stores sell gifts by mail. Many gift manufacturers will drop-ship orders to your customers. Some people have become millionaires and many others have increased their income yearly by selling mail-order gifts.

Baby Items. Consider the millions of families with babies, and you can see the excellent profit potential for these products. In the U.S., there were over four million new babies born in a recent year. Add the global birthrate to this, and you get some idea of the size of the international baby product market. Closely related to the baby market are bride items, which include gifts for weddings, engagements, and showers.

Do-It-Yourself Kits. These products enable people to redecorate, to clean, to install, to repair, or to do any other activity on their own. Look over some mail-order ads to see what types of kits are currently being offered. Do-it-yourself kits will always have appeal. Many people will continue to want to fix, clean, construct, sharpen, mold, or whatever themselves.

Camping, Sports, and Recreation Items.   As you read these words, there are millions of people everywhere dreaming about their next camping trip. Camping equipment ranges from basic gear to expensive items. Sleeping bags, backpacks, cooking gear, and special clothing for camping are just a few possibilities you might keep in mind. Camping is the most popular type of vacation, and you might just be able to cash in on this interest via mail order. As for recreation, the Owens-Corning Fiberglass Corporation reports that recreation and sports have shown a pattern of consistent growth over the last ten years. A whopping $25 billion was spent last year on motor homes, sailboats, and tennis rackets—a rise of $15 billion from ten years ago—and a continued growth in the coming years is expected.

Self-Defense Products.   The rapid and continuing increase in crime has made self-defense a most profitable mail-order category. The *Wall Street Journal* reports that self-defense products are in demand and offer a great opportunity today. These products include clubs, chemical guns, and special canes that virtually turn into swords with a flip of the wrist. Several psychics have predicted that crime will continue to increase for the rest of the century.

Toy Balloons.   A first display ad for toy balloons brought mail-order millionaire Joseph Cossman thousands of dollars. Greatly encouraged, he plowed more money into advertising and sold close to $500,000 of the balloons in one year alone.

Dolls.   Some mail-order firms have done amazingly well selling inexpensive and unique dolls at bargain prices. Doll tie-ins with films like "Star Wars" are popular and sell well.

There you have them. These types of product items have done well for their owners, and many of them are still being sold successfully today. Perhaps one of these categories will be the key to your own first product selection and successful start in mail order. Refer to this list often for product ideas. Ask yourself what each category suggests in the way of a product or service. Focus on those product categories that interest and enthuse you the most.

The product categories already given are those that have sold well in the past. The following list of products includes those items that are presently being advertised in leading mail-order magazines like *Popular Science, Specialty Salesman,* and *House Beautiful.* Notice that these products also fall within the categories already cited. Some of them are simply updated versions of previous products. Others are old staples—products that sold well years ago and because they continue to bring in orders are still being offered today.

1. Books on solar energy
2. Colonial curtains
3. Dollhouses
4. Tablecloths
5. Coin banks
6. Portable ironing boards
7. Address labels
8. Exercise aids
9. Puzzles
10. Burglar and fire alarms
11. Spare-time moneymaking activities
12. Plans to cut the cost of gas
13. Instructions on winning contests
14. Beds for dogs
15. Coonskin caps
16. Grandfather and cuckoo clocks
17. Porcelain plates
18. Replicas of Navaho rugs
19. Household inventory books
20. Body-building courses
21. Patent information booklets for inventors
22. Family crest rings
23. Baby catalogs
24. A variety of mail-order plans
25. Indian jewelry
26. Lace curtains
27. Steel screwdriver
28. Folding tables
29. Special lamps

Part II
ADVERTISING

SUCCESS STORY: Direct Mail Financial Advisory Service

Gypsy Kemp runs a direct-mail financial advisory service from her ranch in New Mexico. She got started, back in 1975, by running a classified ad just to see what the results might be. Her first ad cost her $184 and it pulled such a large response that she continued to advertise her service. Her business now grosses more than a quarter of a million dollars each year. Gypsy spends only four hours a day operating her business: the rest of the time she relaxes with her family or friends or goes skiiing.

5

Advertising Your Product

Before we take a specific look at mail-order advertising, it will help you to understand some key points about advertising in general. Advertising is big business and is growing by leaps and bounds.

What is advertising? Rosser Reeves, in *Reality in Advertising* (Alfred Knopf, New York, 1961), states that advertising "is merely a substitute for a personal sales force."

Advertising is a huge industry, employing copywriters, artists, media people, account executives (glorified salesmen), research personnel, and general office workers. Advertising has been flourishing and expanding for over a hundred years. For at least the rest of the twentieth century, nothing but further boom is predicted for the industry.

The lights burn late on Madison Avenue and also in thousands of other offices here and around the world. Someone must work late to get a new ad finished, rewrite a radio or television commercial, or dream up a new campaign theme that will increase sales for any one of thousands of products or services.

Many of the hardest working people in advertising are copywriters. They write the copy for the print ads, the radio and television commercials, and even the billboards. They often originate the campaign ideas or themes that help to put a product over in the mind of the consumer. Copy is king in advertising and remains the vital link in moving the goods and services of a nation.

THE HERITAGE OF ADVERTISING

The American College Dictionary defines advertising as "the act or practice of bringing anything, as one's wants or one's business, into public notice, especially by paid announcements in periodicals, on billboards, etc., or on the radio."

Advertising dates back to the day of the caveman. The precise time when the printed word began to be used in advertising is unknown. But we do know—from evidence in the British Museum—that an Egyptian once advertised for the return of a runaway slave. Various contests, events, and gladiator games were advertised in ancient Rome.

Much of the early advertising got out of hand. There was a lack of ethics. Many false claims appeared in ads. Through the centuries, advertising has matured right along with communications itself. In the last 100 years alone, advertising has made enormous advancement. It stands today as one of the solid pillars of free enterprise.

THE LEGENDARY CLAUDE HOPKINS

Anyone worth his or her salt in advertising knows about the remarkable Claude Hopkins. He was one of the greatest and most successful advertising men of this century. Hopkins was motivated by one dominant drive in all the advertising he created—to sell, to move the product. His book, *Scientific Advertising* (Crown, 1966), written in 1923, became the copywriting bible of the advertising business.

The accomplishments of Hopkins have become virtually a legend. By far the most effective copywriter of his time, he made a fortune. He skyrocketed Schlitz beer to the top of the American market in a way that showed cleverness, as well as good psychology. He focused his advertising on the fact that the Schlitz bottles were "cleaned with live steam."

Today, many years after the appearance of Hopkins and his book, the great majority of people in advertising still agree with his basic conclusions. He believed that a test campaign can answer almost any question quickly and cheaply, that the only purpose of advertising is to make sales, that ad writers shouldn't try to be amusing, that introducing a personality into an ad can make a product famous.

Hopkins felt that advertising is much like the game of chess. He was convinced that a smart copywriter does not attack a rival, but

Somewhere West of Laramie

SOMEWHERE west of Laramie there's a broncho-busting, steer-roping girl who knows what I'm talking about. She can tell what a sassy pony, that's a cross between greased lightning and the place where it hits, can do with eleven hundred pounds of steel and action when he's going high, wide and handsome.

The truth is—the Playboy was built for her.

Built for the lass whose face is brown with the sun when the day is done of revel and romp and race.

She loves the cross of the wild and the tame.

There's a savor of links about that car—of laughter and lilt and light—a hint of old loves—and saddle and quirt. It's a brawny thing—yet a graceful thing for the sweep o' the Avenue.

Step into the Playboy when the hour grows dull with things gone dead and stale.

Then start for the land of real living with the spirit of the lass who rides, lean and rangy, into the red horizon of a Wyoming twilight.

This is one of the great ads of all time. It was a completely new approach to selling cars.

shows the bright side of his product. He tells people what to do, not what to avoid.

He warned of a trap that some copywriters fall into at one time or another, "The only purpose of advertising is to make sales. Ad writers forget they are salesmen and try to be performers. Instead of sales, they seek applause. Don't try to be amusing. Money spending is a serious matter. The more you tell the more you sell."

THE COPYWRITER OF TODAY

To a large extent, today's advertising is psychology in action. Back in the late 1960s, entertainer and advertising genius Stan Freberg shook up the airline industry with his unheard of concept of admitting in ads that many people feel nervous when flying. One of his print ads, for example, showed a nervous executive on a plane about to be airborne. The headline read, "Hey there, you with the sweaty palms." Freberg could have used the same old tired approach. Instead, he brought new honesty into airline advertising by saying that some people don't enjoy flying and get nervous.

Although far too much advertising insults or disgusts the human intelligence, a healthy amount of it entertains, while still getting the message over. A good example of entertaining advertising is the Alka-Seltzer television commercial of a few years ago. It showed actor George Raft and a group of convicts beating on lunch tables while chanting "Alka-Seltzer." The commercial entertained without irritating or insulting one's intelligence.

Today's modern copywriter must keep in mind that there is a real connection between advertising and psychology. A good knowledge of human nature can be very helpful in motivating people to buy various products.

Curiosity, for example, is an important tool of a copywriter. A number of advertised products attract buyers through curiosity. It's a very strong incentive. The cereals Puffed Wheat and Puffed Rice attained success largely through their appeal to the curious. The ad slogan "Foods shot from guns" led both cereals to substantial new success.

There is a great deal of respect today for the intelligent use of psychology in advertising. In general, motivational research is simply the systematic study of why consumers do what they do, why they buy certain products and shun others. Such studies attempt to correlate the buyer's needs, desires, emotions, and actions. The reasons why consumers buy certain products, patronize certain businesses, support specific candidates, and continually choose the goods and services they do stem from human nature itself. By compiling data on what appeals to consumers, motivational research helps the sales-person to find the most effective way to approach the consumer. The following references may give you new ideas for products and ad-vertising appeals as well as some valuable insights into consumer motivation:

- Boyd, Harper, and Ralph Westfall. *Marketing Research Text and Cases.* Homewood, Ill.: Richard D. Irwin, 1972, pp. 617-38.

- Green, Paul, and Donald Tull. *Research for Marketing Decisions.* Englewood Cliffs, N.J.: Prentice-Hall, 1966, pp. 163-77.

- Martineau, Pierre. *Motivation in Advertising (Motives That Make People Buy).* New York: McGraw-Hill, 1957.

- Smith, George H. *Motivation Research in Advertising and Marketing.* Westport, Conn.: Greenwood Press, 1971.

Most authorities on the advertising industry agree that the most important quality an ad can have is believability. Can the consumer visualize himself or herself using the product or service? As one advertising executive put it, "All business is done in the human mind."

Do people really need the vast array of products and services advertised? Pat Steel, a veteran advertising executive, answers the question this way, "People don't really need these things—art, music, literature, newspapers, historians, wheels, calendars, philosophy. All people really need is a cave, a piece of meat, and possibly, a fire." Helen Woodward, in *It's an Art*, states that "the best ads aren't the ones about which you say, 'Isn't that clever?' but the ones which make you take out your pocketbook and buy something."

WHAT A COPYWRITER NEEDS

To really be effective and sell a product or service, a copywriter needs a strong knowledge of the product, a commercial sense, logic, imagination, a keen selling instinct, good judgment, the ability to write, a sentimental streak, plenty of curiosity, prolific ideas, a sense of humor, and a fondness for people.

Perhaps the one element common to most of the better copywriters is previous sales experience. Advertising is a selling business, and everything in advertising is geared to move the product and please the client.

A certain flair for the English language is a definite help. In the words of Bernice Fitz-Gibbon, another advertising professional, "Nothing else will give a copywriter the same surge of self-confidence that knowing the English language will." Obviously, any copywriter should have (or develop) a deep love for working with words. Unless you intend to sell only a few basic products by mail order, you will need to develop good copywriting skills. The more products you sell, the more copywriting you will be planning and writing.

Mark Twain stressed the importance of words in another way: "A powerful agent is the right word. Whenever we come upon one of these intensely right words in a book or a newspaper, the resulting effect is physical as well as spiritual, and electrically prompt."

If you don't feel confident about working with words, don't let it keep you out of mail order. You can learn how to use words effectively, as surely as you learned how to walk as a child. Advertising writing is a craft, and a craft can be learned.

6
How to Save Money on Advertising

YOUR OWN "IN-HOUSE" AGENCY

If you plan to be in mail order for any length of time, you will save money by setting up your own ad agency. Don't let this worry you. It's not complicated at all. Most publications give ad agencies a 15 percent commission, usually in the form of a discount on all ads placed. Choose a name for your own agency and have some separate letterheads printed, and you will be able to save yourself 15 percent. Many people who own and operate a mail-order business place their ads through their own "in-house" agencies.

In starting your business, you would be wise to operate from your home or apartment. Even just a room is okay. You can store your business materials and product stock in a closet, as many small firms do. Go slowly at first and plan your moves in advance. This will save you time and money in the long run.

You will be the one planning and writing the ads to sell your products. And you choose the mail-order publications in which to run your ads. So you've done all the work—not some outside ad agency. If you run fifty or more ads in a year, for example, you'll be able to save a lot by placing the ads yourself through your own in-house agency, and you will have earned the savings.

Before I started running my first ads, I chose a name for my own agency and had a thousand letterheads printed with my agency name and address on them. To avoid confusion, try to pick a name that hasn't been used. Some possible examples are Creative Advertising, Novelty Advertising, or maybe Southern Advertising.

I still do business under my own in-house agency name. I ran a lot of ads during my first year in mail order, so I saved a considerable amount of money. You can do the same. If you ever wish to offer an advertising service, your agency letterheads will come in very handy. In addition to my mail-order selling, I did some advertising copy work for several large companies. These companies have since developed into regular clients. I do advertising, public relations, and sales promotion for them today on a regular basis. So your agency letterheads can be useful in several ways.

Most publications will accept the ads you wish to place through your in-house agency without question. I never had any trouble myself, and my ads have appeared in just about all the leading mail-order magazines. Some publications say they won't accept in-house agency ads, but this is usually said just to keep the recognized advertising agencies content. Such restrictions are seldom actually enforced.

Remember. A mail-order magazine will not give you the 15 percent discount on your ad if you place the ad through your mail-order company. Although your in-house agency is, in reality, only a name on a letterhead it is necessary for the discount. You're doing all the work, so why not place your ads yourself through your own agency and save yourself a little money? You might wish to have a different address for your agency (one different from your regular mail-order company address), but I used the same address for both my agency and mail-order company, and I never had any trouble.

I also opened a separate checking account at my bank in the name of my in-house agency. I then paid for the ads I ran with checks showing my agency name and address. I see no reason why you can't do the same.

WHAT YOU SHOULD KNOW ABOUT YOUR BUYER

Regardless of the product, service, or other offer you sell by mail, you'll eventually come to realize a vital truth about the world of selling today: Today's buyer is very selective.

Why is this so? Why has the average consumer become so choosy about what he or she buys? There are three basic reasons for this characteristic of modern consumers. By knowing these reasons and how they influence today's buyer, you'll have a better idea of how to motivate prospects into sending you an order.

One general reason is that the buyer of today is pretty hard to please. Most of today's buyers are relatively well educated, fairly sophisticated in their likes and dislikes, and, therefore, more selective.

Today's Buyer Is Well Educated

Is it really true? Is today's buyer all that well educated? Yes. Most buyers know a good deal about a lot of things today. They've learned a great deal just from watching television each evening over a period of years.

It's also true that many of today's buyers have either a college education or at least some years of college behind them. Time spent in the armed forces has also added to the overall education of a large number of people. A number of recent studies indicate that the amount of time spent on reading has gone up in many countries, so that the average prospect today is fairly well read.

The fact that the buyers of today are well educated has broad implications. It means that buyers of the late twentieth century are sharp and will probably grow increasingly sharper through the last decades of the century. It's not just book learning between their ears; prospects are wise to the realities and problems of life today. They know who they want to vote for and why, and what kind of prodcuts, services, and offers they're willing to spend money on.

What does all this mean to you, as a mail-order operator trying to interest prospects in your products and offers? It means that the planning behind your advertising strategy must take this high educational level of your buyers into account if you're going to be consistently effective in getting your share of the business.

Today's Buyer Is Sophisticated

Buyers of today are very aware of the value of products and services in general. They're sophisticated about buying. They've learned from both good and bad purchase experiences in the past. They've also been bombarded with media advertisements and commercials, so they've heard or seen literally thousands of commercial plugs and sales pitches. What this all adds up to is a high level of sophistication that comes into play whenever they make buying selections.

Prospects and buyers can be grouped into three categories. To begin with, there's the brainy type of buyer. This type of person is often the hard-boiled businessman. He's rarely, if ever, swayed by his emotions. He uses plenty of deduction and logic to reach his decisions.

Another of today's types of buyers is the emotional person. This type usually gets along well with people, is fond of fancy food, usually dislikes physical labor, and is generally a slow thinker. He is often convinced and sold through his feelings and can become a consistent customer.

A third kind of buyer is simply a combination of the brainy and emotional types. This person is made up of both emotion and thought. This type wants to both think and feel right about any deal he or she is considering.

Unfortunately, your mail-order ads and direct-mail sales letters can't sort out which prospects fall into which of these categories. But if you run your ads in the leading mail-order publications, you can be sure that large numbers of people from all three groups will be exposed to your ads. So your sales messages should be beamed at all three kinds of buyers. Also, if you send out enough sales letters to the people on good name lists, you'll be communicating with all three categories of buyers.

Today's Buyer Is Selective

People may be fairly quick to spend $5, $10, or even $20 for a given product. But most of them will do some real thinking before deciding to buy a $50, $75, or higher-priced item. When the economy of a country goes through depressed economic periods, this naturally has an effect on the buying decisions of most prospects. It makes them more selective.

Although you won't see the prospects who respond to your ads and offers, it's still a good idea to try to keep up with the changing nature of prospects and customers. It's entirely possible for a mail-order operator to know his product well, have a strong series of ads or sales letters, but still lack an understanding of the prospects he hopes will send him an order.

You can rarely know too much about the prospects you're trying to reach and the changes affecting them. You should try to develop a sound idea of the pressures and influences being exerted on your prospective buyers.

SOME SOUND ADVICE FOR YOUR SUCCESS

Remember. Prospects and customers are the lifeblood of your mail-order business. There's always more to learn about them and about ways to communicate your sales message to them more effectively.

Andrew Carnegie gave some fine advice on success. He advised those wanting success to "put all your eggs in one basket, and then watch that basket. Men who do that do not often fail."

There's nothing to prevent you from learning more about the prospects and customers you hope will build your business. Why do some buy and others fail to respond to your offers and ads? Why do some seem to understand and react promptly to your mail offers? The answers to such questions can do a lot to increase your sales and profits.

Some wise and forward thinking mail-order operators include a reply card or return note in the direct mail they send out. They ask prospects to state their reason or reasons for not responding to a particular offer. Naturally, many prospects won't give their reasons, but a number of them do. Such information can be very helpful when planning future offers and direct mailings.

You might consider keeping a continuing diary or observation book in which you write down various notes and other things you learn about prospects and customers. You could call your book *What I've Learned About Selling to Prospects and Customers by Mail*. The idea would be to form the valuable habit of recording the observations and ideas you have gained from dealing with prospects. You might be surprised at how much you can learn by using this method.

So keep it in mind that today's buyer is changing. Just being aware of this fact and responding to the knowledge that the prospects you'll be dealing with by mail are generally sophisticated, selective, and smart make you a better mail-order operator and a more successful one.

MOTIVATING YOUR PROSPECTS TO TAKE ACTION

Having an attractive product or service to offer is vitally important to your success in mail order. But landing the sale is crucial too. Unless you motivate your prospects to take action and send you an order, your products and services won't move. You need a steady flow of orders coming in to keep your business growing.

Can you close enough sales? The answer to this question will determine your degree of success in mail order, regardless of the product or service being sold.

Unlike those who sell to prospects on a face-to-face basis, in mail order you depend on the total effect and pulling power of your ad or direct-mail letter. You don't have the prospect beside you, so you have no chance to answer objections or questions about the offer. Your prospect cannot inspect the product and try it out. The words of your ad or sales letter represent you and your offer. So the overall sales appeal must be strong enough to make your prospects decide to send you an order at once.

A face-to-face salesman or saleswoman develops a kind of sixth sense by knowing just when to close a sale. Not so in mail order. Your ad or sales letter is your calling card. So every word must count. Your prospects must feel a desire to take action. Your offer must arouse their interest, and your ads must make them buy at once.

Think about the big selling job you're expecting your ad or sales letter to do for you. You're expecting your ad to grab attention quickly, to attract interest in your offer, and to motivate prospects to take immediate action. That's a lot to expect. But the fact that many ads continue to produce excellent results in exactly this way is one of the fascinating strengths of mail order.

Effective Ads Call for Action

Truly effective ads that get results call for action. This appeal can be a direct request—even a command—for the prospect to "buy now," "order today," or "send the coupon at once."

This call for action to buy is often mixed with some special incentive or extra appeal, which makes it harder for the prospect to resist buying. Such incentives may be something offered free, or a discount if the prospect buys now. Some kind of free gift is often used as the bait to hook prospects. So try to think of some kind of incentive or extra bonus you can offer prospects if they buy at once or within a certain time period. Many prospects will take action and send you an order because of their desire to get an extra bonus you've offered them. Everyone likes a surprise; they like to anticipate what the gift might turn out to be.

If your product or service offers any extra bonus tie-in, be sure to let prospects know it in your ads and sales letters. You could, of course, spotlight such a bonus incentive in a sales letter because you would have a lot of room to do it. A small classified ad limits how many words you can use, but you can still get this extra incentive to buy in the ad.

A phrase that has worked well for me, in both ads and sales letters, is worded this way: "Surprise bonus gift with your order." I developed this phrase myself, and depending on what kind of offer I was selling at the time, found that it usually doubled the orders I received.

Millions the world over are looking for bargains today. The same thing will no doubt be true in the year 2000 and beyond. When prospects know they're going to get the product or service they order, plus an extra free bonus or gift, they're much more motivated to buy without delay. It's just human nature.

So I encourage you to add some kind of basic incentive to your ads and sales letters. You may not be able to do it for every offer, but use it whenever you can. It will definitely increase the number of orders you receive. To be sure that your prospects know about any extra you're offering, bring it out in the copy of your ads and near the end of your sales letters. The addition of a P.S. at the end of your sales letter is an excellent way to remind your prospects of any gift or extra bonus you're offering.

To help you decide on an incentive to offer, several possibilities are listed below. Refer to this chapter when planning new ads, copy, and offers. Here are some proven incentives that you might use:

Limited Supply. When your product supply is running low, use copy phrases like "order now—while they last." There are lots of prospects out there who will make a quicker buying decision if they believe that your product supply is about to run out. So keep this incentive in mind. People don't like to miss out on a good opportunity or bargain.

Free Gift. This is simply an offer of a free gift to each prospect who sends you an order. A ball-point pen is a good example, but there are numerous other items that you could use. One of my first products was an informational booklet. I had another shorter booklet printed at the same time—on a closely related subject. I used this shorter booklet as a free gift and received many comments on it from satisfied customers.

Whatever you use as a free gift, be sure that it isn't too expensive to obtain. You don't want a free gift incentive to eat up all the profits from your basic offer.

Special Offer or Price-cut. There are other ways to say this same thing—such as "clearance," "markdown," or "half-price"—but in all of these the idea you're getting across is that the prospect can get your product or offer at a lower price. This savings appeal is a strong one and is used every day in marketplaces throughout the world.

Free Catalog. This assumes, of course, that your business has developed to the point where it's both wise and practical for you to produce a catalog. The offer of a free catalog is appealing to many prospects. It often works well for items that can be ordered again and again. A catalog increases your chances of making sales, for many of today's modern catalogs offer quite a variety of items.

Free Guide Sheet. This can work well if your basic offer or product is in the informational category. I once tried to sell a guide sheet directly from an ad. Orders were not what I had hoped for, but the guide sheet worked very well for me later as an incentive gift. I have used guide sheets successfully as free gifts many times.

Here is what I believe would be an excellent idea for either an incentive gift or product item itself. A recent study revealed that the average family now takes 2.8 vacations a year plus an average of 7.6 weekend trips away from home per year.

My idea is a booklet or guide sheet that would provide basic vacation tips and information for families. It could include pointers on house or apartment security when on vacation, information on resorts and hotels, the best times for vacations, things to do on vacation, side trips, and the like.

Used as either a primary product or free incentive gift, I believe prospects would be pleased with such a vacation guide. A booklet of this type would require a lot of research and writing, but it could be planned and written up as a one- or two-page guide sheet in practically no time at all.

Price Rise. This is a variation on the savings angle. As a mail-order operator, you are free to lower or raise the prices of your products and services as you choose. Just as prospects are motivated to buy when you lower a price, they will also buy before a rise in the price.

So, for an extra incentive, be sure to let prospects know in your ads and sales letters when the price is about to go up.

Special Benefit. Products become especially important to prospects at times because of some government announcement, national trend, or current timeliness. A good example is a snow and ice scraper. With winters becoming more extreme and dangerous, such items are in greater demand than ever. A special benefit thus serves as an extra incentive to buy a product or service.

Guarantee. This one has already been cited as an important way to increase the number of orders you receive. It belongs in this list because it remains one of the strongest incentives to buy of them all. Be sure to use it in most of your offers. Set a time limit if you wish—for example, a ten-day, two-week, or thirty-day guarantee.

There are other possible incentives such as a free sample, introductory offer, or a prize with every order. But the above list will give you some incentives that are used regularly in mail order. They will help to motivate your prospects to send you an order at once.

I greatly increased the number of orders for a music guide when I offered prospects a free bonus gift. I didn't say exactly what the bonus would be, referring to it only as a "bonus gift." I see no reason why you can't do the same. What your own bonus gift will be is up to you. Even items that don't sell well might be used as gifts or bonus extras to induce prospects to buy from you. You will learn a lot by trying out different incentives.

Never underestimate the importance of curiosity. Prospects may send you an order or a request for more details out of curiosity. Many will simply want to know what your "bonus gift" is, or what your free sample is like. Curiosity is a powerful motivator. Your basic offer must, of course, be clear and specific, but it's fair game to whet a prospect's curiosity regarding any extras you offer. Incentives will increase your business. Use them.

THE TRUTH ABOUT GETTING FREE ADS

During my early months in mail order, I ordered several manuals and booklets on how to succeed in the business. In a number of them, I read a pie-in-the-sky description of how to get free ads for any item I sold by mail.

I'd like to warn you about this free ad talk. Free ads are apparent-ly a widespread myth of the industry. The search for them certainly proved to be a complete waste of my time, postage, and effort.

I kid you not. I followed the instructions and tips on how to obtain free ads exactly. I did just as the manuals instructed. In one system for getting free ads, I was directed to send cover letters containing my requests for free ads to 100 leading magazines. I did just that.

I typed all my cover letters and envelopes for the 100 magazines myself, to save the time and expense. I was brand new to mail order, and I believed what the manuals on the business had said about it being entirely possible to get free ads for my product.

I can only say that I learned the hard way. My cover letters and envelopes were sent to 100 publications and were typed neatly and professionally. I used my letterhead. I described the product I was selling and hinted in each letter (as instructed in the manuals) that I expected to be advertising my product in the future and might decide to use their magazine.

The idea behind free ads, as explained in the mail-order instruction manuals I bought, was to let each publication know that, as a mail-order operator, I wished to test the pulling power of their publication. If results proved good, the first free ad they gave me could lead to a good amount of additional paid-for advertising.

Many of the how-to-succeed-in-mail-order manuals painted a rosy picture of how easy it was to get free ads and how everyone and his brother in mail order had gotten their mail-order companies off to a fine start through many free ads. I was warned to be prepared to handle the flood of cash orders I would be receiving after my free ads had been published in these top magazines.

I can sum up the total results of my campaign for free ads in one word—zero. After following the directions exactly and sending my request letters to 100 magazines, not one free ad was allowed. I was disgusted. More than that, I was plain mad at the mail-order operators who had sold me the manuals on getting off to a great start in mail order through free ads. I had paid them good money for false information. To this day, these same manuals and booklets are being sold to newcomers to the business.

I learned a lot from my experience, of course. What may sound good on paper may not work at all in actual practice. Maybe some do succeed in getting free ads, but I don't think it's through the use of the so-called systems I read about. I made up my mind then that if I ever wrote a book about mail order, I would tell the truth about the way the industry works and expose the myth of free ads.

I remember thinking, when I first read about free ads, that it seemed hard to believe that a national magazine would give a new mail-order operator a free ad. But, maybe a national magazine would want to lure new mail-order companies into the fold with the bait of a free first ad. If returns were good and the first ad pulled, those mail-order firms would continue to use that magazine with paid ads.

I had a good first product that was already pulling for me in various well-known mail-order publications. And I had followed the suggested steps for getting free ads to the letter. I reasoned that I would surely have gotten free ads, from at least some of the 100 magazines I wrote, if the frec ad system really worked. No such luck. None of the 100 publications I wrote to even replied to my letters.

Publicity Letters

Another variation of the same myth is based on the idea of sending out publicity letters to numerous publications. The goal is again supposed to be a free ad. I know of nobody in the mail-order industry who ever got a free ad in this way either.

Editorial Mention

Some people in mail order do claim that it's sometimes possible to get a free editorial mention of your product and company name and address in a publication. If so, I'm sure that it's never referred to as a free ad. Public relations consultants are, of course, skilled at getting editorial plugs in various publications. New product information and company press releases are frequently used by a number of editors. However, I personally do not know of anyone who ever got a free ad or editorial mention by using the specific directions outlined in mail-order instruction manuals.

I think a much sounder way to get an editorial mention or announcement of your new product would be through the proven services of a respected professional public relations agency or consultant. It would cost you a fee, I'm sure, but it might prove worth it.

There's nothing to keep you from writing your own product press releases and sending them to a few national publications. Some magazines do have a new product department and often a special editor who handles this kind of material.

I once phoned the editor of a popular magazine to ask about this business of free ads. He denied the whole idea of free ads and said that his magazine had never allowed any. He did state that new products were sometimes announced in one section of his magazine. He said that I was welcome to send in some brief information about my product, but that he couldn't guarantee it would be used.

I think the timing of an information release is very important. If your new product information arrives at the right time and the particular publication isn't overloaded with such material, you might well get an editorial mention.

A WARNING

I hope you'll proceed slowly and cautiously in the early months of your business. It's fine to look over various instructional materials on how to build your business. But as I've tried to indicate in a number of places in this book, you just can't believe everything you read today.

Of course you're welcome to try contacting major magazines in an effort to get them to mention your new product and your company. You may come up with some way to interest a publication in what you have to offer by mail. Publications, for example, will frequently run an article about a company or a new product that has wide appeal. But I advise you not to use the term "free ads" when communicating with publications. Refer, instead, to product releases and editorial mentions.

I worked hard, carefully following the instructions for getting so-called free ads. I've reported the dismal results. I think you can do far better by starting with classified ads that you pay for. In this way you're sure to get results.

I believe that both the good and the bad sides of the mail-order business need to be reported, and I've sought to cover them in this book. There's a lot of misleading information floating around about all phases of the business. The fact that a manual claims to offer information on building your mail-order business is no guarantee that the information in the manual will be correct. What sounds good on paper may not be workable in actual practice at all.

You'll at least be ahead of many other newcomers to mail order from a close reading and study of this book. Before spending any of your money on a so-called system to get "free ads," ask for proof in the form of names and addresses of other mail-order operators who got these free ads. I, myself, have come to believe more than ever that you don't get something for nothing in this world. You pay for what you get in one way or another.

INCREASING YOUR PROFITS THROUGH ADVERTISING

The key to rising profits in mail order is to have one product, service, or offer bringing in orders and showing a healthy profit, and then to expand advertising by running ads for this item in more publications.

Let's say, for example, that after some good test results, you run your first ad in the "Window Shopping" mail-order section of *House Beautiful* magazine. The item you're offering is a T-shirt with a motto or word on it. Your ad appears in the January issue of *House Beautiful* and pulls beautifully for you. You receive several hundred orders and realize a handsome profit over and above the cost of the ad, your expense in producing or obtaining the shirts, and mailing them to each buyer.

You're in. You're at that happy point of knowing you've got a salable product that prospects will respond to by sending you orders. When you reach this point, it's only simple logic to realize that by advertising the T-shirts in other mail-order publications you can bring in a lot more orders. This is exactly the way that many newcomers to mail order have built their businesses and done exceptionally well.

So in our example, if your ad for T-shirts pleased you with its strong results in *House Beautiful,* your next step to build more profits would be to run the same basic ad in as many other publications as possible.

If you're uncertain that your ad will pull well in other publications and you'd rather expand slowly, you can simply run the ad in four or five more publications. Then if your ad makes a strong showing by bringing in more orders, you can rest assured that you've got a winner. At this point, you can do any one of three things:

1.   Continue to increase your advertising slowly by running the ad in four or five more publications each month or so.

2.   Grow fast. Plow a large amount of your profits into more

advertising. Run your ad in thirty or more publications simultaneously.

3. Take the cautious approach. Maintain a steady level of advertising, by keeping your ad in the same number of publications. In this way, you can tell how long the ad will continue to pull. It can be very helpful to know how many months your ad will continue to bring in orders. Then you can be more confident before jumping into a lot of publications at once.

Bear in mind, too, that most magazines are published once a month or twelve times a year. If you run your ad in each monthly issue of twenty different publications, this means that your ad will be appearing 240 times. Still another way to increase the total effect of your ad would be to run the same ad twice or more in the same issue. Should you run the same exact ad so many times? Why not, as long as it keeps pulling a healthy number of orders for you. An alternate choice is to run slightly different versions of an ad in the same issue.

One very successful mail-order operator runs a small classified ad for a course on writing short paragraphs for money. His ad is short—only a few lines—so he can easily afford to run the ad in a lot of different mail-order publications. I've seen this ad for paragraph writing just about everywhere. The ad must continue to sell because I've seen it for twenty years in hundreds of different publications month after month. This same ad appears three and four times in some issues of leading mail-order publications like *Popular Science, Popular Mechanics, Outdoor Life,* and *Specialty Salesman.*

So when you have a winning ad, stick with it. Don't change it as long as it continues to pull orders or requests. Never change a pulling ad until you're certain that its pulling power has ended.

MAKE YOUR OFFERS SOUND POSSIBLE TO ACHIEVE

Obviously, there must be a huge market still virtually untapped for selling instruction courses, manuals, and systems. There's some sound psychological thinking behind these very successful products. As mentioned earlier, most paragraphs—especially short ones—don't sound hard to write. Many people can see themselves succeeding at writing them—and cashing checks for them. This kind of offer sounds entirely possible to accomplish. Small paragraphs are certainly easier to dream up and to write than a complete article or story.

So whatever you offer prospects, try to focus on items that are workable and realistic. Don't make your offer too complicated or involved. Most people have an A-B-C manner of thinking; they can understand two or three basic points at a time. You'll lose many customers with highly technical or intricate materials. Keep your products and instruction materials easy to understand and use, and you are likely to make more sales.

I highly recommend that you send requests for free details on a variety of courses, instruction manuals or booklets, moneymaking offers, and products. Once you receive the sales literature, read over it, and you'll quickly see that the best-selling items make it sound "easy to write for pay," "easy to double your income in real estate," and so on. Take your cue from these best-selling offers. Keep your own offers easy to understand. Make them look very workable in the minds of your prospects. If you can do this, you'll get a lot more orders and make much more money in mail order.

Part III

MARKETING YOUR PRODUCT OR SERVICE

SUCCESS STORY: Joe Sugarman

One of the kings of the mail-order business is Joe Sugarman, who sells high-priced micro-electronic products. He uses full-size ads in leading publications and has become one of the richest operators in the mail-order industry.

Sugarman studied electrical engineering at the University of Miami. To help a local restaurant increase its customers, he wrote an ad for the school paper, which proved to be so successful that Sugarman soon found himself helping other local businesses through his own small ad agency.

In the early 1970s, Sugarman raised about $12,000 and began to sell a small calculator that worked on a new circuit. He advertised the calculator in the Wall Street Journal and in two weeks he counted a $20,000 profit. He used big display ads, and his calculator kept on selling. He later ran ads in many major magazines and in three months he realized a handsome net profit of $500,000. Sugarman hired some employees and opened an office and a warehouse in Northbrook, Illinois. His company now employs about 50 people and has become the top seller of home burglar alarms and digital watches.

7

Selling Your Product Directly From an Ad

As a newcomer to mail order, your first objective is to get one item pulling orders for you and bringing you a profit. Your next goal will be to gradually add other items to your first proven one. This is the very way most successful mail-order businesses have developed.

In the majority of cases, a new mail-order operator will sell his or her first product item directly from an ad. This method is one of three main ways of selling your product or service. The other two ways are the inquiry and follow-up method and the direct mail approach. In ads the asking prices for products and services should be adjusted periodically to reflect inflation.

It's also possible to have others sell your product from a catalog, which you plan, produce, and distribute to prospects. But at this early stage in your business, you shouldn't even consider a catalog. You'll need time and experience before using a catalog. A catalog also requires that you have a number of products or services to offer prospects. At this point, you should think about one or two items at the most, unless you already have some good mail-order experience and knowledge.

CLASSIFIED ADS

You'd be surprised at how many mail-order businesses were started with small classified ads. These little ads are set in type by numerous mail-order publications. They bring in orders. The first few words or short opening phrases of the ads are capitalized, in order to grab the

99

reader's eye and attention. Here's an example of an attention-getting opener for a classified ad offering a way to stop smoking:

SAY GOODBYE TO CIGARETTES!
Proven way to stop smoking.
Send $4.00 to (name of company and address)

A classified ad has no illustration or artwork with it. The ad consists of the best "selling" words (the fewer words the better) that state what the offer is, the price, and the address where the product or service can be obtained.

You might be wondering whether these small ads can really pull in paid orders on a consistent basis. They certainly do just that, providing the copy is right. Classified ads have been pulling orders for many years. Some individual mail-order operators have received as much as $5,000 in orders from their very first ad. But the product or service offer has to be right, at the right price, in the right publication, and advertised at the right time.

SELLING DIRECTLY FROM AN AD

If you decide to sell your first item directly from an ad, be sure that your asking price for the product is not too high. Anything over four or five dollars will probably be too high. You will often see higher prices quoted in ads, but it would be wise to stay on the safe side with your first product.

In your ad try hard to get across the idea that what you're offering is a bargain. Again, a price of several dollars suggests to a prospect that the offer may be a bargain. This is especially true if the item is something that cannot be found in stores and is not being offered by other mail-order firms.

The following are examples of ads that sound like bargains:

50 Different Foreign Coins, $3.00.
(company address)

Garage Sale Kit. Everything needed for
successful sale. Includes signs, stickers,
tags and booklet. $1.75. (company address)

Another advantage of low-priced items is the simple way in which the offers can be stated. The first ad shown above states the offer in just four words. This is the type of brevity that saves you money.

But if you were trying to sell some involved investment plan or perhaps a correspondence course, you would need a lot more copy to describe the item.

If you want to sell your first product straight from the ad, but the item is priced at five, seven, or even nine dollars, you can still try it out. Some people in mail order disagree with the idea that only low-priced items can be sold from an ad. Although you need more space and words to describe your offer, your ad just might pull enough high-priced orders to return a good profit. But, generally speaking, your chances of a good return will be improved if your offer is priced between $5 and $10. Some even feel that $5 to $7 is high enough.

Here is a checklist to help you determine if you should sell an item directly from a classified ad:

1.   Is the item low priced? (from $5 to $10)

2.   Does the item sound like a bargain? Can you get this idea across in a few well chosen words?

3.   Is the item something people need? Often repeat items like a printing service, address labels, or office supplies are preferable. But it's more difficult to establish an item that must be ordered again and again.

4.   Does your item offer genuine value that will leave your customers satisfied?

5.   Would your item interest a lot of prospects? If the offer is too specialized, you would be better off not trying to sell it from an ad.

6.   Is your item something different or unusual? This novelty effect might put it over big for you. Ask yourself if there's some way you could give your product or offer a novelty effect.

If you can give a yes answer to the above six questions, you probably have an item or offer that can be sold with some success directly from an ad.

As a further help to you in deciding whether to sell an item directly from an ad, here are some ads currently being seen in the classified sections of reliable mail-order publications. You might compare an item or offer that you're considering with some of these.

Notice the few words used to describe each offer, the idea of a bargain, and the low prices quoted.

Parents: Help Your Child Obey! Booklet, send $1. (address)

1,000 Embossed Business Cards $7.35 Postpaid. (address)

How Intelligent Are You? Self-scoring test reveals I.Q. in minutes. Only $2.50. Guaranteed. (address)

Exotic Flaming Main Dishes and Desserts! Fifteen easy recipes $2 plus s.a.s.e. (address)

European Travel! Terrific Tips! Save time, money. $1.50. (address)

Be a Winner! Proven Nationwide Horseracing System. Send $2.50 to (address)

Complete Divorce, Marriage Laws All 50 States. $2.00. (address)

Record producer helps beginners make own commercial recording. Send $3.00. (address)

Learn to Type! Complete information with phonograph record and keyboard makes it real easy. $5.98 Complete. (address)

How to Win Contests! Amazing new booklet reveals 15 winning secrets plus suggested form and letters. Satisfaction guaranteed. $2.00 Ppd. (address)

Eight Hamburger Recipes from Around the World. $1.50. (address)

200 Worldwide Stamps 25¢. (address)

Hangliding. Information package, $1.00. (address)

Genuine Australian Opals. 0.50 carat $6.50. (address)

25 Simple Formulas Can Make You Money—
all 25 for $1.00. (address)

Make Big Money with C.B. Related Product.
$2000 monthly. $2.00. (address)

"Trap" Yourself to Success! $12.95. (address)

Only the last ad on the list has a high price. Many of these ads sound like bargains and are no doubt pulling orders.

SOME GOOD REASONS FOR USING CLASSIFIED ADS

Here are some of the main advantages of using a small classified ad to introduce and advertise your product or service:

1. Classified ads are a definite bargain. The price per word has risen in recent years, but big established mail-order companies continue to use these little ads because they pay off handsomely both in new orders and in names.

2. Classified ads don't require years of advertising knowledge and experience. They are generally easy to plan, write, and place in mail-order publications. Your skill at writing the copy for them will grow quickly.

3. Many mail-order firms actually got started in the business with these little ads, offering one or two items.

4. A classified ad is a fine way to test a new product idea without spending a lot of money.

5. You can learn the basic advertising appeals—in a do-it-yourself way—through classified ads.

6. Nothing is required for these little ads except the wording you want to use.

7. A classified ad enables you to get your product or service message in the pages of a mass-circulation magazine reaching a million or more people. The larger the circulation, the greater the chance that your ad will be seen by buyers interested in your offer.

8. By using classified ads you can set your own rate of growth.

9. You can quickly increase your profits on an item that's pulling orders for you by running more classified ads in other mail-order publications.

10. Classified ads can also be used to obtain the names of prospective buyers. By offering to send free information on your offer to those who write and request it, you can keep well stocked with new names.

WHERE TO RUN YOUR ADS

A question you'll need to answer many times in your business is where to run the ads for your product or service.

Here is a partial list of the leading mail-order publications. The addresses are not given because of location changes that take place occasionally. Also, some magazines go out of business, and others come along. You will find, however, that most of these magazines and some of the newspapers (especially the tabloids) are very effective publications in which to run your first ads.

Many mail-order professionals continue to use these known mail-order publications for the items they launch. You can find the addresses of these publications in *Writer's Market* (published each year). You can also find most of them in the New York Yellow Pages since most of the names on this list are magazines located in New York City. There are a number of other publications you could also use. But the following are some of the best:

- Selling Direct (Atlanta, Georgia)
- Salesman's Opportunity Magazine (Chicago)
- Income Opportunities Magazine (New York)
- House Beautiful Magazine (New York)
- Flower and Garden Magazine (Kansas City)
- American Home Magazine (New York)
- Better Homes and Gardens Magazine (Des Moines, Iowa)
- Grit (Williamsport, Pennsylvania)—newspaper
- Capper's Weekly (Topeka, Kansas)—newspaper
- Fate Magazine (Highland Park, Illinois)—occult magazine

The Mechanics-Electronics Group

- Mechanix Illustrated (New York)—magazine
- Popular Mechanics (New York)—magazine
- Popular Science Monthly Magazine (New York)

- Popular Electronics Magazine (New York)
- Radio Electronics Magazine (New York)
- Elementary Electronics Magazine (New York)

Outdoor Publications

- Outdoor Life Magazine (New York)
- Camping Journal (New York)–magazine
- Sports Afield Magazine (New York)
- Field and Stream Magazine (New York)

Tabloid Newspapers

- The Star (New York)
- National Enquirer (Lantana, Florida)
- Globe (West Palm Beach, Florida)
- National Examiner (Rouses Point, New York)

Miscellaneous Publications

- Popular Photography Magazine (New York)
- The Workbasket Magazine (Kansas City)
- Farm Journal (Philadelphia)
- Modern Bride Magazine (New York)
- Audio Magazine (Philadelphia)

These publications will get you off to a good start. In time, you will come to know which magazines or newspapers are right to use for which kinds of products. The mechanics and electronics magazines, for example, are known to pull well for auto-type products, items with male interest, and various how-to-do-it offers.

One of the very first things you should do, when starting your mail-order business, is to look at the mail-order sections of some of these publications. This way you can see for yourself what products and services are being offered and advertised. You can find most of these publications in the larger libraries. University libraries usually have many of them. Or you may write directly to the publications requesting sample copies. Address your letters to the Classified Advertising Manager.

SOME ADS ARE DOOMED FROM THE START

A mail-order product may have a great series of ads behind it, but unless they're seen by the right buyers nothing will happen. As obvious as this rule may seem, it ranks at the top of the list of reasons why some products don't sell as well as expected.

Much more research and study are needed to determine the reasons why people remember one product and forget others. Some of the larger companies are doing something about this need for more research. Holiday Inns, according to a key executive, has created a broad research-marketing plan, which includes such areas as media and motivational research. At this writing, detailed studies are underway to determine just which media is best for a given type of advertising and why.

The logical question that an advertiser is faced with is "Why don't sales go up?" Mail-order operator X comes up with an effective series of ads. They are placed in the right publications. Then why don't sales move up to the expected minimums? The experts say that four out of five new products are doomed from the moment they leave the drawing boards because they're placed in the wrong magazines and newspapers, or on the wrong radio and television programs. More and better research provides the key to stronger pulling ads.

The point here is that you shouldn't get discouraged if your first ads don't pull as many orders as you had hoped. You'll need time to develop stronger copy for your ads. You will be learning about the various mail-order magazines and which ones are best for your particular offer. Perhaps your first product or service offer isn't right or doesn't have enough appeal. The next product may be a different story. You've got to hang in there and experiment a little. Trying out other new offers can be the step that eventually leads to a successful and profitable business for you.

PLANNING THE COPY FOR YOUR ADS

Copywriting for your mail-order ads will be more fully covered in chapter 8. But here are some specific pointers on planning the copy for your ads—after you have decided where and when to run them. You can refer to this guide in working out your first classified ad. Here are the pointers:

1. Take a sheet of paper and write down all the benefits and

facts about your product or service. Study your list of product facts and try to come up with a central selling idea. This might be just a few words or a key phrase. What you want is something fresh—a main selling point about your product. Some examples are

> "The taste that beats the others cold"
>
> "Things go better with Coke®"

For a mail-order classified ad, you'll need something short and snappy, and a selling point that sparkles.

2. Create an opening attention-getting line for your ad. This will be your headline, the first words of which are usually capitalized and/or printed in bold type. David Ogilvy, a highly respected advertising professional, says that "five times as many people read the headline of an ad as the rest of the words." So hit them hard with a good headline.

3. Make every word in your ad count. Give facts that will make a prospect want to buy.

4. Make your ad a me-to-you message—as if you're communicating with only one person.

5. Mention in the ad whether the asking price is postpaid or whether an extra amount is required for postage. Many ads ask for a small amount of money for sending details on an offer. You'll get more replies, however, if such details are offered free.

6. Keep the words of your ad as simple as possible. Study classified ads regularly looking for examples of simplicity. Make it easy for prospects to understand your offer and to send you an order or request for details.

7. Include the price of your offer and your address. Most classified ads end with the address of the company and a key (a system to indicate which ad brought in the orders).

8. Offer a money-back guarantee on anything you sell, for it usually increases the number of orders you receive. Some experienced pros in mail order, however, believe that the word "guaranteed" may be losing some of its power. So many things are guaranteed today and have been for many years. The word may not be as powerful as it used to be.

9. Be aware that a low-priced item (five dollars or less) will usually take a smaller amount of space and copy than a high-priced item or offer.

10. Make no changes in the copy until orders have fallen off considerably and you're sure that the ad has run out of steam.

11. Try to write copy that appeals to the mass audience.

12. Get someone with a knowledge of advertising to help you if writing the copy for your ads is too troublesome. If you use a recognized advertising agency for help, try to pick one that has had a considerable amount of experience in mail order.

13. Make the promise of your offer as clear and specific as possible.

14. Use attention-getting words in your copy. Some of the most powerful words in classified advertising copy include the following:

    • Free   • How to
    • Valuable   • Now
    • Amazing   • Easy
    • Secret   • Unique
    • Limited Supply   • Weekly
    • Exciting   • Guaranteed

15. Think of copywriting as the art of seeing a product or service in a fresh way.

16. Present the benefits of your offer in a variety of ways. Look for new and effective ways to describe your product or service. Make every word pull its own weight in your ad. Small classified ads can bring you a steady supply of orders and money, so take the necessary time and effort to plan and write them effectively.

THE IMPORTANCE OF KEYING YOUR ADS

One term that confuses newcomers to mail order is "keying an ad." Briefly stated, a key for an ad means a simple way of identifying orders pulled in by a particular ad, so you can know how many orders each ad has produced. This is clearly important information to have.

You might think of a key for an ad as a code you use to discover how much business your ads are pulling for you. The truth is that some copy will do better for you than others. So it helps to be able to spot which ads seem to be the winners for you. Then you'll know which ads to keep running.

The kind of key to use is a decision you must make when you plan and write the copy for your ads. Once you've sent your insertion order to a publication, you usually cannot make any changes in or additions to your ad. This is especially true if a set date for any and all changes has passed. So be sure that each ad you send in has a key. This system is especially helpful when you're running a number of ads in different mail-order magazines or newspapers.

There are different ways to key an ad. You can choose the ones you like best or even think up your own method of keying. Here are some of the usual types of ad keys:

1. A key with two parts. One or two letters, for example, are used to indicate the publication. A number follows the letter or letters to show which monthly issue of the publication the ad appeared in. So this type of key would look like the following:

   SD-3 (SD stands for *Selling Direct,* and the 3 means the March issue.)

   If your ad appeared in the *National Enquirer*, this type of key would look like this:

   NE-8 (Since the *Enquirer* is a weekly newspaper, the 8 would mean the eighth week.)

2. Another way to key an ad is to use a "Dept. No." in the address you give. In other words, each publication in which you advertise is given a different number. "Dept. PM" would then stand for *Popular Mechanics Magazine*. "Dept. HB" would be your code for *House Beautiful Magazine*.

3. You can use different booklet, bulletin, or folder numbers. This kind of key usually works well when prospects are writing you to request more details and information on your offer. To use this method, you would use wording something

like the following in your ad: "Request Booklet L" or "Ask for Bulletin S."

4. You can use different post office box numbers with each number standing for a different publication. This might present problems, however, unless you live in a small town and can make arrangements with the postmaster to use this system. You will probably need his okay to do it, unless you want to actually rent out a number of different boxes.

5. After the address in your ad, you could use "Studio A" or "Studio 1" using any letter or number you like.

6. You could use various code names to stand for different offers or products and the publications in which they appear. But with a growing variety of offers or products and services, this could easily become very complicated. Remember. As your business grows, you will want the easiest way to keep up with the results of your ads.

You might come up with your own ideas about how to key the ads you run. There are some other possibilities. Try to use a basically simple system and one that allows for ample growth of the number of ads you run and offers you introduce.

When you're running only one or two ads, you obviously don't have much need for a key, but if you intend to keep advertising and running various ads in a growing number of mail-order publications, a definite way to key your ads will prove to be very helpful.

As the orders and requests for details come in, you can quickly determine which ads are bringing in the best business and the most orders. You'll also be able to spot the ads doing poorly and yank them to try something else.

Examples of Successful Classified Ads

A good thing about using letters and numbers in your key is the fact that they allow plenty of room for more advertising. If you number 1 to 50 or use the letters A-Z, you will have a system that can be used to identify many different publications.

One of the chief beauties of keying is that it lets you test new ads in various publications. With your key you can be certain which copy works best and in what publications. So key your ads. You'll be glad you did when you're advertising several different items in a dozen or more mail-order publications.

A WORD ABOUT TESTING ADS

Testing is invaluable in the mail-order business. It makes it possible for you to separate the winning ads—the order producers—from the losers. You'd be surprised how many newcomers to mail order have run a few ads, been disappointed at the results, and thrown in the towel.

Let's face it. Unless you're a born advertising genius with a natural feel for the art of motivating prospects to take action, you're going to have to be content—like most others—to grow in the business over a period of time. It's very possible to get rich quick in mail order, but you would be wiser to aim at slow but steady growth.

So, if your first few ads prove to be duds, don't let it throw you. Don't be stampeded that easily out of what could eventually become a most lucrative business for you.

Testing Can Be Your Insurance

Testing new ads, new copy ideas, and new offers can be the one action step that insures your continued success in mail order. It teaches you what will and won't work.

Mail-order publications will charge you so much per word. This amount is usually several dollars a word, depending upon the publication and its reputation for getting results for mail-order companies. When you're spending several dollars a word, it's critical to have some advance idea of the results from an ad before going ahead and running that ad in numerous other publications.

Here are some helpful rules and tips to follow when testing an ad:

1. You can't be sure if you have a winning product or offer until test results prove it.

2. Remember. Your product or offer might be good, but the copy you're using to sell it might be wrong or too weak. So test the offer and also the copy.

3. One quick way to test is to run your ad in a newspaper. Although most of them are not known as very reliable mail-order pullers, newspapers do bring quicker results than monthly magazines. A number of mail-order professionals test in the *New York Times*. Some of the Sunday magazine sections published by various newspapers are a good place to test. Results come in fairly quickly.

4. If the results of any test are poor, you may not have to scrap the item or project after all. Maybe you can redo it. Rewrite the copy, or improve the offer itself. Most of the successful people in mail order seem to have an ability to do this or they develop the skill to do it. After rewriting your ad or improving the basic offer in one or more ways, you might get much better results on the next test.

5. When results are poor, and few orders or replies are received, it could mean that the root of your trouble lies in the product or offer itself.

6. A good way to test copy is to run different advertising copy on the same offer and in the same publication. Then you can see which piece of copy does the best.

7. Remember that you can test the different classifications of a publication (the headings under which your ad appears). You can run one ad under "business opportunities" another one in the "moneymaking opportunity" section, another in the "do-it-yourself" category, and so on. Generally speaking, one of the best places to run your ad is under the "business opportunities" heading. It has a reputation for pulling well. But ask yourself what heading would logically bring the best results for your offer. Then try it.

8. One reason for poor test results may be the fact that too many other mail-order firms are offering the same item or something very similar to it. If too many other mail-order operators are selling your offer, your orders or replies are going to be cut drastically.

9. If you can obtain a well-qualified list of prospects with a

known interest in your type of item or offer, you might try a test mailing via direct mail. Direct mail is also a good way to keep your product or offer private for a while, until you can estimate the reaction to it.

10. Try to avoid testing in the wrong publications. Study the mail-order sections of some of the publications already named. This will give you an up-to-date knowledge of the kinds of offers and products being advertised in which publications. If you can afford it, test in the better mail-order publications. As mentioned before, however, tests in some newspapers and Sunday magazine sections bring quick results.

11. Choose the best issue in which to test a particular ad or offer. Generally speaking, the September, November, and January issues of leading mail-order publications are the three best pulling ones. The September and January issues are especially good. Some product items and offers, however, can be advertised with good results in any month. It depends on what you're offering. The mail-order business usually falls off in the summertime, but it picks up again in the fall. January is usually a very strong pulling month for all kinds of offers.

12. A strong and attractive headline can make a real difference in the test of an ad. Experiment with new headlines when you test. Sometimes a better headline can double your replies.

13. The right list of names in a direct-mail test can mean the difference between success and failure.

14. You can also test different prices for your products and offers. Watch the price you quote carefully. If it's higher than other mail-order dealers are asking for similar items, it will cost you a lot of business. An offer may pull much better when the price is either raised or lowered. A higher price is sometimes identified with better quality. Test to find out what price works the best. Round dollar prices are usually best for lower-priced items ($2, $3, $5).

15. If the results of a second test of an offer are also poor, you should probably drop that item and try something else. But, if you still have faith in it, try to improve the offer or the ad. And run a few more tests.

DETERMINING THE COST OF YOUR CLASSIFIED ADS

How much money does it take to advertise these days? The answer depends on where you run your ads and how often you advertise.

You are charged a set rate for each word in a classified ad. At this writing, the rate for an ad in *Popular Science* (a strong mail-order magazine) is $8.00 per word. By the time you read this, the rate charged could be even higher. A twenty-word ad in *Popular Science* could cost you $160.

The total bill for your ad would be a bit higher if you choose to have the headline of your *Popular Science* ad appear in boldface type with all capital letters. Any additional words you use over the twenty would also be another $8.00 a word.

But look at what you would get for your twenty-word ad in *Popular Science*. Circulation is large—currently 1,800,000. This should mean a good response to your ad. Close to two million people will see the magazine. You can't count on that many seeing your own ad, of course, but the higher the circulation in a reliable mail-order publication, the better the chances that your ad will pull well.

Remember. You pay for the total number of words in a classified ad. Everything in the ad counts. Single numbers, initials, abbreviations, or groups of figures all count as one word each. Most publications count the zip code used in your company address as one word. A few will let you use your zip code free of charge.

To give you an example of how the word count and cost are figured, here is a classified ad that has always done well for me whenever I've run it:

HOW TO BECOME A SELLING ARTICLE WRITER FAST! Guide sheet $1.00. Wilbur Enterprises, 203 N. 10th Street, Murray, Kentucky 42071.

Most publications count the above ad as twenty words. If I ran it in *Popular Science* today, it would cost me $160. I was teaching in a college in Kentucky when I ran this ad for the first several times.

Notice that by omitting the word "street," in the above ad, one word could be saved. Leave out "street," "avenue," or "drive," whenever you can. It will save you money on your ads. Most mail is delivered safely without these extra words in the address.

Here are some more examples of correct word count:

Fred E. Smith	(counts as three words)
P.O. Box 7	(counts as three words)
U.S.A.	(counts as one word)
South Bend	(counts as two words)
1979-1980	(counts as two words)

If you should be incorrect on the exact word count and charge for your ad, the classified advertising department of the magazine you deal with will let you know what additional amount you owe. So don't worry about it. But in most cases, you'll be able to figure the exact cost of your ads.

Just to give you an idea of relative costs, the current rate for a display ad in *Popular Science* is $445 for an inch of space. Even *Popular Science*, itself, states in some of its advertising aimed at mail-order advertisers that "dollar for dollar, classified ads are more profitable than big display ads." So its probably best to stick with classified ads until your business has grown and you believe display ads are justified.

Consider Other Publication Rate Choices

If the *Popular Science* rate of $8.00 per word is too high for you, there are other good mail-order publications that you can use at lower rates. *Popular Mechanics* is a strong pulling choice. Its current rate is $6.25 per word—$1.75 lower than *Popular Science*.

Popular Mechanics will set the first word of your ad in boldface at no extra charge. And the use of your zip code is free too. So a twenty-word ad in *Popular Mechanics* would cost you just $125 which is $35 less than the same ad run in *Popular Science*.

The best way to plan and determine the cost of your classified ad is to write to the publications you're thinking about using. Ask them to send you information about their classified rates. They'll be happy to send you a rate card and full details about their circulation, service to mail-order companies, and pulling power. Advertising is their business, and they want your patronage.

Try to form the habit of planning your ads well in advance. Most mail-order publications require that your classified ad copy be sent to them with full payment by a certain deadline date for each issue.

Say, for example, that you wish to run a classified ad in the May issue of *Popular Mechanics*. The copy for your ad, just as you want it to appear, must be received by the magazine by March 10 in order to be published in the May issue. By writing to each publication and requesting full advertising details, you can obtain specific deadline information for each issue and be certain to have your ad in on time.

When writing to publications for information and advertising rates, address your letter as in the following example:

Classified Advertising Manager
Popular Mechanics Magazine
224 West 57th Street
New York. New York 10019

Publications sometimes move so be sure that you use the correct and current address. Most large libraries have up-to-date issues, so you can always check out the current address, if in doubt.

After you have written to the publications for the first time, you'll have the names of the classified advertising managers, and can address them personally from then on. It's a good idea to keep all advertising rate information in a special file, or, if you wish, you could set up a separate file for each mail-order publication in which you expect to be advertising.

Minimum Number of Words Required

Most mail-order publications require a minimum insertion. By this they mean that they will not accept any ad with less than a certain number of words. The minimum number of words required at *Popular Mechanics* and at most other publications is ten. This is no problem. When you think about it, it's almost impossible to state what your offer is and give your company name and address in a few words. Even when you try to scrimp on words to save money it's hard to write an effective ad in less than 25 words.

I've run ads with fewer words—ten in some cases—but they didn't pull nearly as well as those ads with more words. It's possible to get good results from a brief ad if you're advertising a catalog or an item that requires only a few words. Experiment to see what number of words works best for you.

ESTABLISHING CREDIT FOR ADS

After you've run a number of ads in the same publication, you'll find it possible to establish credit. When a magazine has seen that you've paid for your previous ads in advance and that you appear to be a reliable and regular customer, they may allow you credit on future ads.

With credit you can pay for your ads after cash orders have started to come in. This can be a big help to any mail-order operator because it lets you run many ads without having to pay in advance for them. In this way, you can eventually have many ads appearing in a variety of mail-order publications.

Most publications will send you a complimentary copy of the issue in which your ad appears. This is proof that your ad was published.

Another Way to Save Money on Ads

Many mail-order publications offer what is known as a "frequency discount." If you run more than one ad in the same magazine, you can usually get a discount on the total charge as a reward or inducement to advertise in that publication. Three or four ads run in succeeding issues can save you money, so ask about this when you contact various mail-order magazines.

SENDING IN YOUR AD INSERTION ORDERS

Once you've planned your ad and figured the cost, you're ready to submit your copy to the publications you have selected.

An insertion order is your communication to a publication to run an ad in one issue. There are three basic ways you can send in your order. They are

1. Fill in the classified advertising order form provided by the magazine. When you first write to various mail-order publications for their advertising rates, they will send you a special form for sending in your ad copy.

    Beginning with the fifteenth word or so, many publications will even figure the cost for you in advance. You have only to type in the words of your ad exactly as you want it to be published, and enclose your check or money order for the ad. Many publications will let you charge the cost of your ads.

Be sure that your company name and address are on the form before mailing it. If at all possible, type in each word of your ad neatly. Typing makes your copy easier to read. You want every word to be clear, so there will be no mistakes in the final published ad.

2.   A second way to send in your order to run an ad is to draw up your own special form to use whenever you run new ads. Have enough copies of your form printed so you won't run out. A hundred or so would be a good initial supply, unless you expect to be doing a great deal of advertising.

Use your mail-order company letterhead (or, if you have one, your in-house ad agency letterhead) for this order form. Near the top—just beneath your company name—leave some space for the name and address of the publication you're sending your order to. See Figure 7-1.

You can arrange the information on the form in any way you wish, but it's a good idea to include most of the divisions shown on the sample form. A classified advertising manager or assistant can then tell from a glance at your form what you're advertising, who you are, the heading you want your ad under, the issue you want it in, the number of words in the ad, and the exact copy for the ad.

Near the bottom of your form be sure to have the following words: Total Amount Enclosed for This Ad. After you've filled in the information for each ad you order, the last thing you do is type in the amount required for the ad, as you have figured it. Then simply enclose a check or money order when you send the form.

By completing one of your own special forms for each ad insertion order you send to a publication, you'll be making it very clear what you want done regarding your ad. You can use a carbon when you type the form, so you'll have a copy for your own records. A publication might lose your order form or even your payment for an ad. It happens now and then. So a copy of your order form can be very helpful at times. And you can refer back to it when reviewing ads you've run or checking copy you've used.

3.   A third way to send in your ad instructions is to type a short business letter to the classified advertising manager. State the

THE JOHN BROWN COMPANY
1716 Bluford Street
Phillipsburg, N.J. 08865
(201) 766-9453

(Insert name and address of publication)

Product Advertised: (state nature of product—booklet, service, etc.)

Heading: (Business Opportunities, Do-It-Yourself, or other category)

Publication in Which Ad Is to Appear: (name of publication)

Date Ad Is to Appear: (issue date or month ad will appear)

Number of Times Ad Is to Be Run: (one or more times)

Key: (type in your code for the ad)

Number of Words in Ad: (total number of words)

Copy for Ad: (leave enough space so that all the words of your ad can be

neatly typed)

Rate Per Word: (insert the rate per word charged by the publication)

Total Amount Enclosed for This Ad:

15 Percent Agency Commission
(include if you are using your ad agency letterhead)

Figure 7-1

Tips on Doing Layouts

Keep the layouts for your ads simple and sensible. If they are too complicated and confusing, your prospects may be lost. You want your prospects to become intrigued by the copy of your ad. So make layouts as readable as possible.

Some mail-order firms use both small classified ads and much larger display ads to sell their products and services. You might wish to use both some day, as your business begins to develop and grow.

8
Let's Write a Classified Ad

Now sharpen your pencil and get out some paper. Make yourself comfortable, but keep your thinking cap on tight. You're about to write a classified ad.

I'll be your guide along the way as we create a classified ad together, starting from just a single word or a headline.

This could be one of the most valuable chapters in the entire book for you. You're going to discover how much fun there is in creating a classified ad. But finding the best way to sell a product or offer is also a real challenge.

Creatively speaking, it's stimulating to work up an attractive classified ad. But again, remember that what you want is not to entertain the prospect or to show how clever you are. Your only goal must be to choose and use the strongest selling words. You want words that will make prospects send you an order at once.

COPYWRITING PRINCIPLES TO GUIDE YOU

1. Use the element of curiosity in your ad, for it is a strong human incentive.
2. Realize that people in general want bargains, but they do not want cheapness.
3. Learn some principles of psychology.
4. Offer identical products in different ways.

5. Be aware of the drives, emotions, and attitudes of consumers.

6. Know that consumers don't always think or act as they say they do.

7. Realize that writing ads is a craft that can be learned through practice.

8. Write copy that is easy to read.

9. Concentrate on one main theme.

10. Use emotional appeals in your copy.

11. Employ the four steps of effective copy—attention, interest, communication, and action.

12. Make your ad understandable.

13. Put a time limit on your offer, for it often works well.

14. Use copy phrases that stimulate action ("Free details").

15. In small classified ads, concentrate on facts. (You don't have room to persuade.)

16. Know your product inside out before you write the copy.

17. Keep good copy ideas flowing.

CHOOSE A MAGNETIC HEADLINE

The following true story shows that great ideas for headlines are anywhere and everywhere.

There's a man named Leroy in the Midsouth with a real talent for repairing shoes. He now owns his own store, after working for others for years. He's a friend of mine and has kept my own many pairs of shoes in top condition.

With the price for good shoes now running at over $50 a pair, I've been glad I know this skilled shoe man. I frankly resent having to pay $50 or $60 more today for the same basic shoe I used to buy for $25 or $30 just a few years ago. I think it's a rip-off.

So one day I told Leroy how much I appreciated his keeping my shoes in top shape for such a reasonable price. He keeps them looking and working like new or better.

In gratitude to Leroy, I decided to try to come up with an ad idea he might use to increase his business. I knew that many people would be delighted with his service, once they knew about it.

So I started trying to think up an attractive headline for an ad that Leroy could run in the local paper or even use on a sign in his store window. Here is the headline I created:

Leroy Keeps You Walkin' Happy!!

I walked into Leroy's store one day and hit him with this headline. He was delighted.

"That says it all about what I do for a living—about my business."

"Right. You've kept me walkin' happy now for several years, Leroy. And I'm grateful. So are my feet for that matter."

"That's the kind of line I could use just about anywhere."

Leroy thanked me. And I left his store that day glad that I could show my appreciation for his good service.

My reason for telling you this little story is that it shows the appeal of a strong headline. As an opening line, "Leroy Keeps You Walkin' Happy" could be the start of an effective ad. It would also make a most attractive billboard sign.

Here are some brief pointers about headlines in general. Try to remember them whenever you're looking for a strong opening line.

1. A catchy headline is memorable.

2. The best headlines are usually short. Never have too many words in the opening line.

3. Prospects want to know what a product will do for them. A headline can often sum up the benefit to the customer most effectively.

Now let's assume, just for example, that you've developed a booklet to sell by mail. It's an $8.95 booklet that would have strong appeal for women looking for an executive position and to other women seeking to reenter the job market. You wish to sell the booklet directly from an ad. With such a booklet as your product, how would you write a classified ad to sell it? This is your first assignment. What would you use as a headline for your ad? You might jot down any ideas that come to mind right now. We'll start and complete an ad for this booklet. Before we do, I want you to think about it some. Take a day or two if you wish.

TRY TO AROUSE INTEREST IN A FEW WORDS

If your objective is to get prospects to request more details, you can often do it in a very few words. If your goal is to sell something directly from the ad, it will take more words.

To stimulate your thinking, here are some examples of mail-order headlines. They are taken from current classified ads:

- Identification Card Sales Kit!
- How to Borrow Up to $25,000 Without Interest!
- Fastest, Easiest Piano Course in History!
- Start Used Car Brokerage Business!
- How to Start a Resume Writing Business in Your Spare Time!
- Build $3,000 Foam Plastic Home in One Week!
- Mail-order Millionaire Helps Beginners Make $500 Weekly!
- Free Report: "Executive Type Business"
- New Luxury Car Without Cost!
- Get Rich Using Legal Rip-offs!
- $1,000 Monthly as Publisher's Agent!

Now let's match headlines for the booklet geared for those women who are looking for an executive position. I hope you came up with a strong line that opens your ad, commands attention, and offers your prospects the promise of value for their money. Here are several headlines I came up with and believe would be strong openers:

Women—How to Land that Executive Job!
Land an Executive Job—Whatever Your Age!
Wealth and Status Can Be Yours Too!

Remember. Your goal in writing a headline is to get across the *promise* of what you're offering as quickly as possible. Prospects want to know what's in it for them—what it will do for them. How does your own headline compare with the three suggested above? Maybe you did better than you think.

Do you believe my own three headlines would grab a woman's attention, as she scanned a mail-order classified ad section? Certainly those women who are interested in a career—and there are millions of them—would want to read beyond these headlines to find out more about the offer.

Ask yourself if your own headlines would grab the attention of such women and make them want to know more about your offer. You may have come up with several strong headlines for the booklet. If so, try to choose the one you feel would do the best selling job. You could, of course, run several ads with different headlines for the booklet. But, if you were just trying one ad at first, which of your headlines would you select?

When some of the ads you run don't bring the results you want, you might try switching the headline. Sometimes a change in the headline can improve the pulling performance of an ad.

The next step in our ad for the booklet is to describe the product. In other words, let your prospects know what the product will do for them. The headline of our ad has implied the promise of the product. So now make the nature of the product clear. Is it a course, a device, a service, a novelty item, or what?

So the second line in our ad might be something like this:

New booklet tells how.

A variation of this second line could be as follows:

Proven plan reveals system.

If you used "proven plan," it wouldn't make it as clear to prospects that the product being offered is a booklet. So it would be wiser to substitute the word "booklet" in place of "plan."

Now we have two lines for our booklet ad. Using the second headline (of the three), these lines are:

Land an Executive Job—Whatever Your Age!
New booklet tells how.

The price of the product or offer usually comes next, along with some type of guarantee. There are several ways this could be stated in our booklet ad. Here are some of them:

Only $8.95—guaranteed!

Rush $8.95 (guaranteed) cash or money order to

$8.95—one month guarantee!

If you wish to have a time limit on a guarantee, you might want to state it in the ad, like the third line above does. If the guarantee is ten days or two weeks, you should say so.

I'll bet you can guess what comes next in our ad for the booklet meant for women seeking a job. That's right. A call for desired action. Without such an appeal to prospects to take action, by sending you an order at once, an ad would be stripped of one of its essential elements. Make it a definite rule from the start in your business to always appeal for immediate action.

So this action appeal in our ad could be any of the following lines:

> Order today!! Sterling Enterprises, (key and address of company)
>
> Write: Morrison Company, (key and address)
>
> Act Now!! (company name, address, and key)

Now let's put all of these lines together to make our total booklet ad:

> **Land an Executive Job**—Whatever Your Age! New booklet tells how. Only $8.95—guaranteed! Order today!! Sterling Enterprises, 789 Oak, Dept. PS4, Miami, Florida 39871.

There's our complete ad for the booklet. PS4 stands for the April issue (4 meaning the fourth month) of *Popular Science* magazine.

Not bad. Who knows? The above ad might just be a winner. It does have some good appeal and all the ingredients for pulling orders. The total number of words is 25 (24 if the zip code is allowed free). Notice the exclamation marks in the ad. Use them in your ads, for they give an added effect to the total ad and make it longer when published. The use of "street" or "avenue" was also omitted in order to save one word.

Now let's do another ad for this same booklet product. But this time we'll use a different headline, description, and appeal:

> **Wealth and Status Can Be Yours Too!** Proven booklet reveals system. Rush $8.95 (guaranteed) cash or money order to: Sterling Enterprises, 789 Oak, Division SS1, Chicago, Illinois 60601.

This last ad runs a few more words—a total of 27, not counting the zip code. By cutting the words "cash or money order," you could save four words and reduce the cost of the ad. This would make a total of 23 words. But you might want to include "cash or money order" in your ad. The decision is yours. You could save another word, by using just one word for your company instead of two.

WRITING ADS TO PULL INQUIRIES

Many experienced mail-order operators have discovered that selling products priced over $5 directly from an ad may not bring the desired results. The sales of our booklet on landing an executive job might be higher if we ran some classified ads meant to bring in requests for details rather than cash orders.

If you chose this route, what would some inquiry and follow-up ads be like? Here are a few examples:

> **Women—How to Land that Executive Job!** Free information. Vista- 1, 203 Oakdale, Dallas, Texas 78431.

Not counting the zip code, the above ad runs only 14 words. Notice how one word—"vista"—is used. "Vista" could be used here as a key to stand for this particular booklet being offered. The number one after "vista" could stand for the publication in which you're advertising.

Let's try another inquiry and follow-up ad and see if we could make it even shorter:

> **Women—Land that Executive Job!!** Free details. Success- PM, 899 Willett, Boston, Mass. 01237.

The ad comes to only 13 words or 14 if you count the zip code. Again, the word "success" could be the code key for the booklet being sold. The letters PM mean that the ad was run in *Popular Mechanics* magazine. If additional ads were run, a number after the letters could indicate which issue was used.

It's perfectly alright for you to try selling a product both directly from an ad and also by the inquiry and follow-up method. Once you learn which selling method pulls the best, you can stick with that choice. Some products priced over five dollars sell fairly well directly from an ad. You'll have to test specific products and prices. As a general rule, however, items sold directly from an ad will do better if kept under five dollars.

The point is to not get at all discouraged if a product you try selling directly from an ad does poorly. If the price you're asking is over six dollars, you might just get prospects to send you requests for details by running small ads like the above and following up with sales literature. Of course, you would then need a sales letter to send back to the prospects to persuade them to send you an order.

It's a good idea to actually write several different ads for each product or offer that you plan to advertise. You'll gain some excellent experience by creating small classified ads, and your chances of coming up with a strong ad will be improved.

Never believe that any particular ad you write is the best you can do. The more ads you create, the better you'll become at it. Copywriting is a developed skill; it improves with time and practice.

By now, you no doubt realize that small classified ads require a short but punchy style. What you're trying to communicate are the basic facts about your product or offer, so a prospect can quickly decide to send you either an order or a request for more details.

DON'T UNDERESTIMATE THE POWER OF CURIOSITY

Curiosity may have killed the cat, but it does human beings a world of good. Stimulate the curiosity of your prospects through the ads you run, and your future in mail order will be successful and profitable.

"Curiosity is, in great and generous minds, the first passion and the last," said Samuel Johnson. For one thing, people in general, and prospects in particular, are more alive when they're curious. This desire to know more about a variety of things is very important.

Curiosity can be an enormous help to you, in the writing of classified ads or any other form of advertising. Start forming the habit now of being curious about which selling approaches to use, which headlines may pull the strongest, which prices for your offers are the right ones, which publications are best suited to your products. The answers can mean more money in your bank account.

How Curiosity Led to a Recorded Song

Curiosity once led me to visit one of the most awesome and historical battlefields of the Civil War—Shiloh National Park. I became fascinated with the place and read more about the battle fought there.

In time, I found that I wanted to return again and again to Shiloh, to stand beside the Bloody Pond, to gaze at the cannons now standing silent in the fields, to walk the River Road where Grant walked and planned his military strategy, and to see again the trenches where northern and southern soldiers were buried together.

The result of my visits to the battlefield and my thoughts about what happened there was a song I wrote about Shiloh. My song, "Shiloh," was recorded and released nationally, receiving strong reaction and comment from the key radio market areas. The song brought me mail from just about everywhere.

Remember. Curiosity is often the reason why many prospects will send you an order for your product or a request for additional information. Strive to stimulate this vital element of curiosity with your ads, and it will pay off for you in more sales and inquiries about your offers.

As an example of using curiosity in a classified ad, I once offered a hefty booklet on building a career in the world of music. Since my asking price for the booklet was $9.95, I decided that it would be best to advertise for inquiries. I worked out a two-page sales letter and had a good supply of copies printed.

I was then ready for my ad to appear. Here is the ad as it appeared in many leading mail-order publications. Notice the element of curiosity in the headline:

> **Secret Plan** Puts You in the Music Business! Free information. Write today!! (my company name, key, and address)

The ad brought in hundreds of requests for more details. I sent a sales letter to each prospect telling more about the booklet. After the sales letter was received by the prospects, I began to receive orders. The ad brought me a handsome profit whenever I ran it. I still offer the booklet today, and the above ad never fails to bring in a large number of inquiries.

Naturally, many of those who wrote to me for more details responded out of curiosity. Look again at the headline of the ad, especially the first two words, "Secret Plan." Let me assure you that one of the most powerful selling words in mail order is the word "secret." There's an almost magical quality about this word. Use the word "secret" in your own ad copy whenever you can, if it fits the nature of your product or offer.

I told the truth in my ad. The booklet I offered was indeed a secret plan that would enable the buyer of the booklet to actually get into the music business and build a successful career. I still receive mail today from satisfied customers who bought my career booklet. I'm sure that some of them used the information in the booklet to get into the fascinating music industry. But it was the words "secret plan" that first attracted many prospects to send me a request for free details.

So, if and when you develop some type of informational booklet to offer by mail, look for words and phrases to use in your copy that will appeal to a prospect's curiosity. It's true, of course, that a request for more details may not mean a sale. You will also need a sales letter to motivate prospects to send you an order (see chapter 11).

You may be wondering if I could have sold my music booklet directly from an ad. Because my asking price was $9.95 (postage paid), I reasoned correctly that most prospects would want more details on the booklet before sending me almost $10. I could have gotten orders directly from an ad, but I'm sure that I did much better by using the inquiry and follow-up method.

Prospects need to be sold more if you're asking them to send you $10 or more. Mail-order buyers may not hesitate to send you a few dollars (up to $5 or so) in direct response to an ad, but when the price is $10 or more, they usually need more convincing.

In the long run, I advise you to use the inquiry and follow-up method if your product or offer is $7 or more. I think the overall results will be better for you. Use your own judgment if your asking price is $5 or $6. You might try out both methods as a test.

THE SENSE OF NEWNESS AND EXCLUSIVENESS

What about the sense of newness generated by a mail-order product? Buyers everywhere like to know that they're getting something new for their money. They enjoy thinking that a product they order by mail cannot be obtained in regular store outlets.

Many ads and sales letters for mail-order products and services do, in fact, call attention to the exclusiveness of their product. The ads often make a major point of the fact that the particular item being offered cannot be bought anywhere else. This approach increases the lure of the product. Buyers, in general, want to order a product all that much more if it is exclusive.

WORD POWER

Whatever your goals or objectives may be in the classified ads you write, stay well aware of the great power of words. The copy you use in your ads can not only increase your immediate income, but it can also help you establish your mail-order business and keep it consistently successful.

Whether you want to get the elements of surprise, newness, curiosity, or value into your ads, words will serve as the major tool of your business. You can pay an ad agency or someone else to write ads for you, but there's a lot to be said for developing a basic skill with words yourself.

If you want to stay in mail order for years to come, one of the smartest things you can do today is to fall in love with words. Learn how they can work for you in all kinds of ads. A skill with words in the copy you produce for your products or services could bring you a steady and comfortable income for life—maybe even make you rich. Strong selling words make for effective ads. And strong ads bring in lots of orders.

Sigmund Freud once summed up the great power of words most effectively: "Words have a magical power. They can bring either the greatest happiness or deepest despair; can transfer knowledge from teacher to student; words enable the orator to sway his audience and dictate its decisions. Words are capable of arousing the strongest emotions and prompting all men's actions."

One way to become more aware of the strongest selling words in ads is to circle the powerful ones and clip the entire ads out of magazines and newspapers. Then save these ads in a special file for future reference.

Now here is another project for you. In the two ads below, circle the strongest words—the ones you believe do the best job of selling. It's alright if you choose several from each section of copy. The first one is from a display ad. The second is a classified ad. Here they are:

> **HOW TO WIN CONTESTS!** Amazing new booklet reveals 15 winning secrets plus suggested forms and letters. Satisfaction guaranteed! $2.00 PPD. (company name and address)

SUCCESS GUIDE THAT MADE ONE MAN WORLD
FAMOUS can bring you better money results too! Only
$2.00. Order now!! (company name and address)

The words I would have circled in the first ad include "amazing,"
"new," "winning," "secrets," and "guaranteed." "Satisfaction" is
also a good one and could be circled.

My best word choices in the second ad above are "success,"
"world famous," "money," and "order now." How many did you
circle? Perhaps you circled most of the same words. Whenever you
see strong selling words in ads, cut them out. This will train your
mind to be on the alert for them.

CREATING AN AD FROM ONE WORD

As one final example of how a classified ad is created, let's think up
another product and do an ad built around just one starting word.

This time, let's say that the item you wish to sell is a game about
the world of politics. For the sake of example, let's call this game
"Candidate." The asking price for the game is $7.95—guaranteed.

Now here's your assignment. Write a classified ad from either of
the words "Candidate" or "play." Starting with a verb as the first
word in your ad is often better than a noun; but a good classified
ad could be started with either word.

Take an hour or so, or an evening if you wish, to try your hand at
writing an ad for this game. Don't look at the ad below until you've
written one yourself, starting with either word. I'll be taking some
time to create an ad myself.

Earlier in this chapter, you created a classified ad from a headline.
That is, you got a headline first. In this case, you have either one of
two words to start your ad. This example is to show you that an ad
can be written starting with just one word. Good luck.

The ad I've done appears upside-down in the footnote so you
won't be tempted to look at it until you've written your own ad.*

*Here is the copy I wrote for the game "Candidate." Compare it with your
own. I started with the word "play." Here is the ad:

(name, key, and address)
and votes. Only $7.95—guaranteed. Order today!! (my company
Play the Game of Candidate Yourself! Wheel and deal for fun

Not bad. The above ad is only 18 words, not counting my company name,
key, and address.

How did you do with your ad? Count the total number of words in it. Practice in writing ads like this is excellent training for your business. Don't expect the first or second ad you write to be perfect. My own ad isn't perfect. Maybe I could do a better one using the word "Candidate" as a starter. You might want to try another ad, yourself, using "Candidate" as your starter.

The idea of urging you to write some ads is to get you thinking about the copy, headlines, and selling words for a variety of products. This practice will be very helpful to you when you're ready to write a real ad for your first mail-order product or service.

Refer back to this chapter often, when you're planning new ads and creating the copy for them. And keep these summary points in mind:

1. Ads can be created from a headline or even a key word.

2. Verbs are often good opening words to use.

3. Strong copy consists of words and phrases that command attention.

4. Make sure your ad offers a promise. Prospects want to know what your product or offer will do for them. Tell them.

5. Be specific. Stress the key facts of your offer.

6. Don't fail to ask for action.

7. Try to appeal to curiosity in your copy whenever possible.

8. Practice in writing classified ads can be invaluable and will help you to become established in your business sooner.

Following are five ad "assignments" for you. You can gain some additional experience by writing classified ads for each of them. Take a few days to think about each assignment if you wish. There's no hurry. Some of these are just fictional product items I've dreamed up to give you more practice in writing ads. A few of them are actually being sold today by mail, so you'll be writing ads for existing mail-order products in some cases. Enjoy yourself. You may well be laying the foundation for a prosperous mail-order career. More power to you.

AD ASSIGNMENTS

1. Write a classifed ad for a booklet on how to quit smoking priced at $4.00. The booklet is guaranteed.

2. Write a classified ad meant to bring requests for more details about a $9.95 inventor's guide. This is an inquiry and follow-up type ad.

3. Write a classified ad for the Sarah Adams Cookbook, priced at $8.95. There's a month guarantee on the offer.

4. Write a classified ad for a $3.95 Highway Safety Kit. The kit includes four large posters requesting help in case of accident, sickness, out-of-gas, and mechanical trouble.

5. Assume that you're a record producer. Write an ad offering a service to beginners instructing them on how to make a commercial recording. The asking price is $4.00. No guarantee is included.

9
The Inquiry and Follow-Up Method

The inquiry and follow-up method means just what it says. You run small classified ads stating your offer. Those who are interested in your offer write to you for more details, and then you send them follow-up literature or information concerning your offer. One big advantage of selling this way is that your original ad—run to get prospects to request details from you—usually requires only a few words. You thus save on the cost of advertising.

Here are some examples of the inquiry and follow-up ads currently running in several leading mail-order publications. Notice that most of them offer to send free information:

Exciting, Moneymaking Opportunity! No experience required! Details 25¢. (address)

CONTROL $1,000,000 IN REAL ESTATE! Net $2,000 monthly! No selling. No capital to start. Unique leverage opportunity. Free brochure. (address)

Start Your Own Correspondence School. Information 50¢. (address)

BUILD YOUR OWN Sofa, Love seat, Chair. Free Brochure. (address)

HOW TO MAKE MONEY in Commercial Art. Information Free! (address)

$50,000 Yearly Possible! Become Financial Broker! Free Details! (address)

Earthworm Profits, Grow in garage, basement! Free literature. (address)

Notice that the first of the above ads asks for twenty-five cents for details on an offer. Some of these ads, designed to get inquiries from prospects, request a small amount of money (usually twenty-five to fifty cents). This money helps a mail-order firm to meet the expense of sending follow-up details to those who request more information. If you receive hundreds of requests for more details, the postage costs can quickly add up. But many interested prospects may not respond to ads that ask for a quarter or half-dollar for details on an offer. Most of the inquiry ads you'll see in mail-order magazines and newspapers offer free information—with no charge or strings whatsoever. The reason for this is that many mail-order operators want new prospect names. And these mail-order firms know that by asking for even a small amount of money they may cut down the number of inquiries they'll receive. Your goal in the inquiry and follow-up method is to develop a growing list of customer names. These names can be valuable to you. Why? Simply because you can sell many different offers to these same names. Many customers will buy from you over and over if you treat them right, fill their orders promptly, and offer good products. Many mail-order firms continually run small classified ads offering free details in order to maintain a steady supply of prospect names. So when you use the inquiry and follow-up selling method, it is best to offer details, information, literature, or brochures for free.

INQUIRY AND FOLLOW-UP IS COMPLICATED

By now you've realized that the inquiry and follow-up method of selling is more complicated than selling directly from an ad. Here are some basic reasons why this is so:

1. Printed sales literature on your product, service, or offer is required. This literature can range from a one-page sales letter to a four-page, two-color booklet.
2. Order forms are needed, so your customers can easily mail you an order.

3.   A circular that sums up your product or offer is often used in sales literature. Mail-order experts recommend the use of a circular.

4.   Specialization is required. This means that strategic copy, illustrations, and a lot of planning are required to describe your offer.

5.   Strong sales literature is necessary for high-priced offers such as correspondence courses, which may range in price from $8 to $100 or more. It's much harder to get a $50 order than a $5 order.

6.   A time lag is involved in receiving orders. Your profits on orders don't come in quickly. You have to send details to those who respond to your ads and then wait for sales.

A GOOD WAY TO LEARN THIS METHOD

I'm a firm believer in learning by doing. I learned a great deal about mail order by testing ads and closely observing the results. I see no reason why you cannot do the same.

If you like the sound of the inquiry and follow-up method and are determined to try it, there's a way you can do it without investing a lot of money. It's the way I first tried this method, and I still use it today for certain products. Here are the steps to follow, as I did when I ran my first inquiry and follow-up ads:

1.   Develop a product, service, or offer at a price ranging from $7.95 to $14.95. In this illustration, as in my own case, the product is an informational booklet. I developed a 45-page report and priced it at $10.00.

2.   Write the report yourself, as I did, or if you don't want to tackle this alone, you can team up with your spouse or other family member, or even a friend or neighbor. Come up with a good subject for your booklet—something that will have great appeal. There are many possible subjects that will sell for you.

3.   Type your booklet neatly, and have some initial copies printed. The more copies you have printed, the more money you will save. Since many offset printers have fairly reasonable prices, you can have 50 or 100 copies printed without spending a lot.

4.   Write a *one-page* sales letter (just like you would write to a friend), and type it neatly. Since you're just trying out this inquiry and follow-up method as an experiment, forget about long involved sales literature. Use a clean, new ribbon for the typing. As simply as possible, tell what your booklet is about and why you believe it will help a prospect. In the last few paragraphs ask for the prospect's order. Near the bottom of the letter leave some space for the prospect's name and address and the manner of payment (see Figure 9-1).

Name (please print) _____

Address _____

City _____

State _____   Zip Code _____

Check _____   Money Order _____   Cash _____

Figure 9-1

Be certain, also, that the full price for your product, service, or offer is quoted somewhere on the order form. If an extra amount is required for postage, say so. If the price is postpaid, then state that on the form. Make it easy for a prospect to send you an order.

5.   Have a few hundred copies of your one-page sales letter printed by offset. Black ink on 8½ x 11 size white paper (a good bond paper) is the cheapest. I usually request a twenty-pound type paper for most of my own printing orders.

6.   Run a few test ads in some good mail-order publications *before* you have your booklet printed to see what kind of response you will get on your offer. Use a few words to tell what your booklet is about and offer to send free details in the ad.

7.   Send your one-page sales letter (with order form at the bottom) to each prospect who requests more details. Be sure to enclose a business return envelope with each sales letter you mail out.

8.   Have your printer on the alert, ready to print your first booklet copies. When you start receiving a number of requests for details, you'll have to decide whether or not to have copies of the booklet printed. A lot of requests for free details means that there's some interest in your offer. Some people will respond out of curiosity, and after seeing your sales letter, may not send you an order. But others will order if your ads have been run in good mail-order publications and if your sales letter has done its job.

I'm not guaranteeing this is a foolproof system. You may get twenty-five or fifty requests for details, and you may receive only a few orders from these after you send out your sales letters. On the other hand, you just might do well enough to recoup your expenses and possibly make a small profit. You will at least be learning this inquiry and follow-up method of selling from actual experience. And if it doesn't work for you the first time, it may work the next time with another offer.

Coordination could be a problem for you. By this, I mean that before going ahead and having the printing done, you've got to find out if your offer is a dud, if it's lukewarm, or if it's a winner. You'll lose money and be stuck with all fifty or more booklets unless you have some idea in advance of how well your offer is going to sell. If requests for details on your offer only trickle in and add up to a disappointing few, you can scrap your plans and save the cost of printing the booklets. You could, of course, have only ten or fifteen booklets printed. Then if your offer doesn't pull well, you're not out as much money. But the cost of printing a few booklets is, of course, much higher than printing a lot of booklets. As a rule, the more copies you have printed the more money you save.

You will have to go ahead and have a one-page sales letter printed to send to each request you get for more details. People who buy by mail don't like to wait too long to hear from mail-order companies. The quicker you can get back to them with details on your offer, the better your chances will be for receiving actual orders.

If your first sales letter doesn't work, you can chalk up the printing expense as valuable experience you've gained. Maybe your second sales letter will do much better.

Orders should also be filled promptly. There's a government law in effect now requiring mail-order operators to fill orders received (to have them in the mail to customers) within 30 days. The law was passed to protect mail-order buyers who order products and then never receive them or have to wait months before they're filled. Customers who send you an order will expect to receive the item within 30 days or get their money back. The sooner you fill every order and request for details on an offer, the better for your entire business. Try to make it an ironclad rule in your business to fill each order you receive within 24 hours.

Remember this. Some offset printers are very slow in filling their printing orders. They get swamped with orders at times, or a holiday period delays printing. So allow enough time for your material to be printed and shipped back to you. You can, of course, save time by phoning your printer to go ahead on a substantial printing order. Some prompt, reliable printers and their current addresses are given in Chapter 1.

IF THERE'S NO RESPONSE TO YOUR SALES LITERATURE

Just because a prospect doesn't respond to your sales literature or letter promptly, it may not mean that you've lost a sale. Send that prospect another sales letter (a duplicate) in two weeks. If there's still no response, keep trying with additional letters every few weeks. On $7.95 to $14.95 priced offers, you should usually hear after the second try, if a prospect is going to buy at all. Higher-priced items may take four or five attempts to get an order.

If the response to your sales literature or letter is poor, you can always either redo it or try an entirely new one. Chapter 11, on sales letters, can help you.

PER INQUIRY SELLING BY RADIO

The advantage of per inquiry selling is that it allows you to see if certain radio stations can produce large numbers of orders for you. If a station is unable to get enough orders, you pay nothing for the air-time used.

This is really a special form of radio advertising used only for certain kinds of products or services. It's still mail order. But instead of your ad appearing in a publication, your offer is advertised on the air, usually in the form of a spot announcement.

In per inquiry selling, you are usually expected to send some information to the station about your product, its benefits, and why you believe it will sell. You offer a discount to the station (about 35–40 percent per order received).

Your radio commercial sales message is announced at certain times on the stations. Orders are sent on to you, after the stations deduct their discount rate for advertising your offer.

I have never tried this form of selling, though I did consider it a few times. I don't recommend it to you—at least not at first. I believe that small classified ads are, by far, the best way to launch your business. You can then go on to both display ads and direct mail.

Some mail-order firms claim they have done well using the per inquiry method, but stick to classified ads at first in your business. Later on, after you've grown a little, you might try a per inquiry arrangement with a few stations if you wish. Not every offer is right for radio advertising, however. Lists of stations that will consider working with you in this way can be easily obtained. These stations often advertise in leading mail-order publications.

SUCCESS STORY:
Music Career Guide

*When I first began to operate my own mail-order business,
I discovered through research that some twenty-five million people in the United States alone are trying to write
songs and place them with music publishers or record
labels. Millions more all over the world are also caught up
in the lure of a music career. I knew music well and had
years of experience in it, so I spent several months developing the idea of a music career guide.*

*I used the inquiry and-follow-up method to get pros-
pects. I first ran classified ads in the leading mail-order
publications and then sent full information on my music
career guide to those who responded. My first few ads
brought an avalanche of requests for more details. I quickly sold out of my first printing of the guide. I still sell it
for $9.95, and it continues to bring in cash orders through
classified ads and also through direct mail. The market for
music products is evidently endless.*

10
Direct Mail: A Dynamic Selling Tool

A major way of selling your product or service is via direct mail. Direct mail is similar to the inquiry and follow-up method because in both methods you use a sales letter or sales literature to sell your offer. But in direct mail you send your sales material directly to a specific list of qualified names. You don't run an ad to get prospects as in the inquiry and follow-up method.

When selling directly from an ad or by inquiry and follow-up, you receive either orders or inquiries, and from these you obtain your supply of prospect names. But in direct mail, you already have a list of names. You send the information about your offer or your sales literature to each name on the list. Those on the list who wish to buy then mail their orders back to you.

Direct mail is very important to your future in mail order. It could eventually become a virtual gold mine for you. This chapter gives you a general idea of what direct mail is about and also explains some of the more important aspects of direct mail in detail.

DIRECT MAIL IN GENERAL

Who uses direct mail? The answer is—all kinds of companies. From large organizations to individuals, many companies use it as a tool to increase the sales of their products or services. Politicians have filled their campaign fund chests numerous times for years through the use

mailing only to 2,000–3,000 names. If the response is encouraging, then you can increase your next mailing to 5,000 or more names. You should go slowly in the early development of your business. If your first test turns out poorly, you'll be glad you didn't go overboard by trying 10,000 names.

Be Suspicious of Mailing Lists

It's wise to be suspicious of mailing lists until you have some substantial proof that their quality is good. With mailing lists selling for cold, hard cash and with so many lists on the market, there's a lot of competition among mailing-list brokers. This competition sometimes results in deceptive sales practices. By not knowing who you're dealing with or what makes a good list, you can waste a lot of money. If the names on the list you use are phony, "deadwood copies," or are copied from other lists, you're going to lose money, time, postage, and hope. So go slowly. Ask mailing-list brokers you're considering for full information on their lists. And check out the broker's reputation and background in the mail-order business. Again, test with small numbers of names at first. Another good test is to send your sales letters to more than one mailing list. Your sales letters may pull great when sent to one list of names and yet do poorly when mailed to another list. The selection of a high quality list is essential to your future in direct mail.

Your Best Mailing List

Your most productive and highest quality mailing list is the growing list of customers who have sent you orders. This list is valuable to you because you can send offers to these customers again and again. If pleased and satisfied with one of your offers, many customers will buy from you again. So your own list of customers can be your best list of potential buyers.

Mailing-List Sources

Here are some good sources for names of potential direct-mail buyers. Following these are names and addresses of some leading mailing-list brokers.

1. Mailing-list brokers.
2. Public records.

3. Membership rosters of organizations and associations. (Some organizations even sell a directory of their entire membership.)
4. Fraternal, civic, professional, and religious groups.
5. Display, classified, and inquiry-and-follow-up ads.
6. Financial rating books.
7. Government lists.
8. Telephone books (names classified in the Yellow Pages by trade or occupation).

Mailing-List Brokers

Names Unlimited
183 Madison Avenue
New York, New York 10016

Dunhill List, Incorporated
419 Park Avenue, South
New York, New York 10016

Dependable Lists
333 N. Michigan Avenue
Chicago, Illinois 60601

National Business Lists
295 Madison Avenue
New York, New York 10017

The Kleid Company
200 Park Avenue
New York, New York 10016

MDC List Management
41 Kimler Drive
Hazelwood, Missouri 63043

THE DIRECT-MAIL PACKAGE

The direct-mail package usually consists of a sales letter, a circular, order form, outer envelope, and reply envelope. Each of these elements of a direct-mail package will be discussed in Chapter 11. Keep in mind that the sales letter is by far the most important part of the total package you send.

SOME EXAMPLES OF DIRECT-MAIL PRODUCTS

Here are some examples of products currently being sold by direct mail. (Some of the products listed can also be sold by the inquiry and follow-up method.)

1. A seventeen-page sales booklet offering study courses such as "Instant Math," "Double Your Reading Speed in One Week," "Instant Memory Power," "Self-Hypnotism," "Listening Concentration," and "Good Health and Vigor after Fifty" is sent

out by Automated Learning, Incorporated. The price for each course is currently quoted at $9.98.

2. A service for inventors is offered by a company in New York. The company sends out a brochure describing the service with an attached reply card. A free "Inventors Information Kit" is sent to those who request it, and all facts and details on the service are offered free of charge.

3. A secret plan for making money is described in a brochure sent out by another company in New York. A free gift is also offered to anyone ordering. The price is $20.

4. A series of reports on how religion can make a person financially independent is offered for $20.

5. A small book on how to be a more effective speaker is offered free to those interested in a course in public speaking. A one-page sales letter brings in requests for the free book.

6. Life, hospital, and accident insurance plans are offered by insurance companies through direct mail. Some of these companies even obtain the birth dates of the people they contact by direct mail. I recently received two sales letters from two different insurance firms. In both cases, the first thing I saw was a policy with my name, birth date, and monthly premium amount clearly stated (they obtain this information from public records). This type of sales letter is clever because it *personalizes* the offer. Both sales letters also stated that the premium can never be raised and that the plans cannot be canceled. There's little doubt that these companies do well with this effective use of direct mail.

SOMETHING TO REMEMBER ABOUT DIRECT MAIL

One great advantage of using direct mail is that it doesn't let all the other mail-order firms know what your offer or product is. Sometimes you may want to see how a special offer will do. And you don't want everyone else in mail order to know about it. Remember. Anyone in this business can see what's being offered by simply looking over the mail-order sections of publications. So keep this privacy factor of direct mail in mind. It can be especially useful when you want to test new offers.

...IL CAN BE YOUR ROAD TO RICHES

...ater, direct mail can mean the big time for your mail-
...ness. Today's newcomer to mail-order may well be one of
...w's high-stake dealers in direct mail. There are sound reasons
...irect mail can be the road to riches for you:

1. You can bring in more responses per thousand pieces of mail
   sent out than by any other medium.
2. You can make your sales package just as simple or sophisticated as you wish. It can range from a one-page sales letter and
   reply card to a four-page, four-color letter, circular, and order
   form.
3. You can test your offers or products more often. Different
   sales letters and combinations of sales literature can bring a
   variety of responses.
4. You can have a fast-growing list of customers.
5. You can focus on only those prospects who have responded to
   offers similar to yours. You thus reach qualified prospects.
   You can also send your mailings only to selected geographic
   sections.
6. You can send out as many offers as you wish. And you can
   time your mailings to arrive at any time you want them to.
7. You can send new offers to your growing customer list time
   after time for extra sales. So you can build a thriving business
   from your own private list of customers.
8. You can have more freedom in what you say in your direct-
   mail copy than you can in ads.
9. You can send your offer to individual names, making your
   sales technique much more personal. Unlike ads, there is no
   arena effect—ads surrounded by other ads. Your prospects
   open their mail and there is your sales message—with no other
   competing ads to lure them away.

On the other hand, you must realize that direct mail is expensive.
This is probably its greatest disadvantage. The average cost of getting
your mailings in the hands of qualified prospects is currently $175 to
$350 per thousand. And postage rates are climbing. The cost of
sending out direct mail is rising yearly. How expensive your direct

L. L. Bean is one of the most successful mail-order companies in the nation.

catalogs carefully and refer to them often. Ask yourself the following questions about each catalog:

1. How many items are offered in the catalog?
2. What is the average price of a catalog item?
3. Are the catalog items guaranteed?
4. Are the catalog items appealing to most people?
5. Are the catalog items available in stores?
6. Are there any items that would stimulate repeat sales and influence customers to buy similar products?
7. Is the catalog printed in black and white or in color?
8. Is the catalog durable enough to hold up to a lot of handling?

Catalog Buying Is Growing

Another reason to begin thinking about a catalog of your own is that ordering by catalog is becoming increasingly popular. The *New York Times* recently reported that "the century old practice of catalog shopping is booming. Consumers representing all income levels and interests (from insurance to correspondence courses) are attracted by mail-order catalogs." Proof of this catalog buying boom is reflected in the Montgomery Ward catalog, which is sent yearly to over six million consumer households.

YOUR OWN MINICATALOG

There's an easy way to get into catalog selling if you insist on trying it. You don't need a thirty-five-page, three-color catalog to bring in orders. All you need is a one-page minicatalog. My first catalog was one sheet of paper listing seven items. The argument can be made that a one-page list of items is not a real catalog. In the traditional view of what catalogs are supposed to be, this is true. But from my own point of view, it is a catalog. So here's the point. There's nothing to keep you from listing all of your offers on a one-page sheet.

Once you decide to use a one-page catalog, have it printed and include it in your regular mail-order package. This is the same way that regular full-size catalogs are sent to prospects. Whenever you communicate with a prospect, send along your one-page minicatalog, and you should receive many additional orders.

Catalog

...entually build a much better catalog from this minicata-
...ng this one-page catalog will get you thinking about cata-
...eral, give you experience in describing your products or
...rove to you that enclosing catalogs brings in extra orders,
...urage you to develop a better catalog in the future. Many
...are developed in this way and have grown from very small
...igs.

...second catalog may need two pages or more to describe all
...r items. From this point on there's no limit to the amount of
...andise you can sell by mail. You should be sure, however, that
...'s a market for each item you add to your catalog. A continuous
study of what's being offered in other catalogs can be a valuable
guide in selecting your catalog items. Most successful catalogs have
one strong characteristic—variety. Although you can't possibly have
something for everyone and will probably never compete with the
Sears Roebuck catalog, try to have some variety in your catalog.

ONE WAY TO A FORTUNE IN DIRECT MAIL

A catalog of your own that continues to expand and grow yearly is
one way to a fortune in direct mail. It often takes years of experience, but fortunes are being made today from catalog sales. Again,
until you have experience in operating your mail-order business, I
strongly urge you to delay any plans for a catalog. You first need the
thrill and encouragement of selling profitably by classified ads. But
keep in mind the idea of one day having your own catalog. It can be
a good ace in the hole ready to play in the future. And who knows?
It might just be the card in your mail-order hand to win you a
fortune in orders.

DIRECT-MAIL SALES LITERATURE

The key parts of a direct-mail package are a sales letter, order form,
circular, and reply envelope. Leaving out any one of these may reduce the number of orders you will get.

Next, we'll take a look at each of the essential parts of a total
direct-mail package. When you decide to try a direct mailing, you'll
want to have a basic understanding of each key element.

11

The Direct-Mail Package

THE SALES LETTER

The most important part of any direct-mail package is the sales letter. Don't ever forget it. The order form, circular, brochure, and reply envelope add extra pulling strength, but the sales letter is the persuasive tool that leads a prospect to send you an order. A good sales letter is like money in the bank.

Millions of people everywhere receive direct mail each week or even daily. A lot of it gets thrown away, but you'd be surprised at how many people actually read sales letters.

If a sales letter can grab attention with an appealing headline or opening, a prospect will probably read the first paragraph of the letter. If his or her interest is still held, most of the letter will probably be read. Getting attention is absolutely vital, and is the first goal of a sales letter.

A sales letter is somewhat like a Seeing Eye dog. Prospects are "blind" when they first open a piece of direct mail; they don't have the foggiest idea what is being offered. But they do know that someone is trying to sell them something. So their sales resistance is called into play.

A friend of mine recently received eight pieces of "junk mail" (as he called them) on a single day. These offers were trying to sell him on buying land in Florida, subscribing to two magazines, increasing his hospital insurance, and receiving a stock investment newsletter.

The point is this. To compete with all the other direct mail a prospect receives in a week's time, your own sales letter or literature has got to be strong. A professional, well-planned sales letter can put your offer head and shoulders above the others. Your offer or product will stand out like a lighthouse in the murky darkness.

How to Make a Good Sales Letter

Here's how to make a strong sales letter:

1. Design an effective letterhead. Few prospects will react to a letter printed on plain paper and without a company name and address at the top. Black and white letterheads can pull orders, but one or two colors usually brings better results.

2. Make your letter sound friendly. Cold and lifeless letters go nowhere.

3. Use letter-size (8½ by 11), twenty-pound stock paper. Again, colored paper is better. In my own business, I found that women prospects respond to the color pink, and men to the color blue, but there's no hard-and-fast rule to this. You can test different colors for both paper and ink to see what works best.

4. Avoid wordiness and long, involved paragraphs. The best sales letters look inviting to read. Underline words for emphasis and indent paragraphs. Keep the total effect of your letter simple. Orders come from easy-to-read letters.

5. Have your printing done on one side of the paper only for best results. But for a four-page letter, you can hold the paper cost down by printing on both sides of a sheet. Some letters still seem to pull well even when printed on both sides and without any colors. It's what your letter says that counts the most. But do try to keep your letter neat and professional looking.

6. Many sales letters still open with "dear friend." You can do the same or skip this greeting entirely.

7. Be as specific as possible when explaining your offer or product.

8. Try to appeal to a prospect's emotions and dominant desires.

9. Use a P.S. at the end of your sales letter. Make this P.S. a strong appeal to action, a reminder of any bonus gift you are

offering, or a fresh wrap-up of your offer. Never underestimate the power of a strong **P.S.** at the close of a sales letter.

You Can Learn to Write Good Sales Letters

There's one path leading to a fortune in direct mail, and it is to develop a skill for writing sales letters that will pull orders. Once you know how to plan and write sales letters that will bring in good results, you can write your own ticket. There are many corporations that will be happy to send you large checks for writing their sales letters. So the ability to write strong sales letters is well worth developing.

Sales letters are big business. Since they are an excellent way to deliver a sales message, many large companies use sales letters consistently to increase their overall profits. You could offer your services to one of these companies. Or you could use this valuable skill for yourself by writing sales letters for your own offers. Some people make money both ways. But keep this in mind: most companies that will give you an assignment to write a sales letter will only pay you a flat fee for your service. This means that even though you get $700 to write a sales letter for a company, that firm might turn around and make a fortune by using your letter.

So when you perfect the skill of creating sales letters, you'd be smarter to use your talent to make money for yourself. One strong sales letter can pull enough orders to raise your bank account considerably. Some sales letters can bring you so many orders that you'll probably have to hire outside help to get all your mail opened. I'm talking about strong sales letters that motivate prospects to send you an order at once. So set a goal now to develop a sharp ability to plan and write sales letters. One thing is certain. Once you have a sales letter that brings in stacks of orders for your own offer, you may forget about classified ads and stick with direct mail from then on. The road to riches in mail order is the ability to write sales letters that keep on pulling orders till the profits literally stagger your own belief.

Ad Copy Versus Sales Letters

You may discover that you can do far better at writing sales letters than you can at writing copy for ads. Some individuals freeze up when they try to sit down and write copy for an ad. Maybe the word

WILBUR ENTERPRISES

1763 *Autumn Avenue*
Memphis, Tennessee 38112

THE BEST JOB IN THE WORLD COULD BE YOURS - CREATING ALL
KINDS OF MONEY-MAKING IDEAS!

Dear Friend:

I'm sure you'll agree that the best job in the world would be one in which you work for yourself, set your own hours, live anywhere you wish, and see your income rise or double year after year. IT COULD ALL BE YOURS!

What could be more wonderful than being paid well to create all kinds of ideas? You're the boss...in business for yourself.

I'm talking about your own creative idea business. I've had my own for over 10-years and see no reason why you can't do the same by following my simple plan.

Millions of people everywhere have to drag themselves to work each day. They dislike their work and feel trapped in a dead-end job. It's a sheer waste of time and human energy.

My simple directions on how to start and run your own creative business can put checks in your mail-box day after day. And finding money in your mail is always a delight!

My plan is no mail-order scheme. There are no ads to buy or run, no name lists to get, no circulars to print or stock merchandise to keep. I fell for such worthless mail-order offers myself years ago and wasted money on them. So I'm not about to cheat anyone this way...or any other.

My plan is a proven way to tap the creative ability now within you and make it pay off for you in many ways. I show you exactly HOW TO increase your creative powers and make them work for you in the form of MONEY-MAKING ideas.

I've been well paid for many years to create new ideas. You can do the same thing.

I'm no tycoon...just an ordinary person who got tired of slaving for other companies, inconsiderate bosses, and working in jobs with little or no future.

I dreamed of having my own business for years. One day I said goodbye to the 9 to 5 life and struck out on my own. I've never been sorry. In fact, I've been much happier ever since. I have complete creative freedom in my

own business. And my business and income continue to grow each year.

I WANT THE SAME THING TO HAPPEN TO YOU. Your success in your own creative idea business will be no competition to mine..simply because there are too many markets all paying well for new ideas. Why should I be greedy?

What ideas do you create? All kinds. Greeting cards (at $25 to $50 per accepted idea), short filler articles easy to do, newspaper and magazine articles—features, art and advertising ideas, new toy ideas, short stories, books, textbook ideas, fashion ideas, songs, poems, TV scripts, new inventions, sales ideas (if you sell anything for a living), and many more.

All the above ideas and more are in demand and pay from $25 or $50 up to THOUSANDS OF DOLLARS and/or royalty contracts.

You send these ideas to the editors and executives of such companies, publications, newspapers, and firms. They're waiting with OPEN CHECK-BOOKS to send you good money for ideas they can use.

The only way you use the mail is sending your ideas to the right places. IT COSTS YOU NOTHING but the time and paper to create these new ideas..plus the postage to send them on their way. You can start part-time now if you wish (for an EXTRA INCOME) and go full-time later.

But first you have to become more creative and alert to new ideas. My proven plan will make you more creative within days. I also name some key places (markets) where you can start sending ideas.

Is it really possible to build a good income with creative ideas? I'm the proof that it is. I've created thousands of such ideas and sent them out all over the world. I've had lots of fun doing it and been well paid.

There's ONE RISK. Once creating new ideas for MONEY gets in your blood, it may ruin you for doing any other type of work. THERE'S JUST NOTHING LIKE BEING YOUR OWN BOSS IN A PROFITABLE BUSINESS THAT'S ALSO FUN!

One more thing. When you send me the enclosed PINK ORDER FORM and a money order, I will send your copy of my plan BY RETURN MAIL. Personal checks take about two weeks to clear. We fill all orders (sent with money orders) THE SAME DAY THEY'RE RECEIVED.

Your satisfaction with my plan is guaranteed or I will refund your money.

Yours sincerely,

L. Perry Wilbur

P.S. My idea business now brings me a monthly annuity...a certain amount of money to start each month. It could do the same for you!

"copy" scares them. Basic sales technique applies to copy for both ads and sales letters, but some people seem to be much better at planning and writing a sales letter. It's easier to be informal in a friendly sales letter. And you certainly have more space in a letter to tell your story than in an ad. You should try writing both kinds of copy. After you've tried both ad copy and sales letters, you may decide to use one exclusively or use both simultaneously.

A Proven Plan for Learning to Write Good Sales Letters

I would like to suggest a plan for learning to write good sales letters that has worked well for me. This plan was developed from a study of the principles of direct-mail selling, the knowledge and methods of successful mail-order operators, and the experiences I have had in writing and using sales letters. The key word in any plan of this type is "practice." Planning and writing sales letters is like playing the guitar—there's always a lot more to learn. You will discover this for yourself as you learn to write good sales letters.

1. Read and study various sales letters that are being used today. A quick way to get these sales letters is to answer a number of ads that offer free details and the letters will be delivered to your mailbox. Before long, your name will be on several direct-mail lists, and you will be bombarded with sales letters and literature for all kinds of products and offers. Watch your current mail, also. You're probably already receiving a number of direct-mail offers. Don't throw them away; save the sales letters for future reference. In a short time, you'll have a thick folder of letters to study.

2. Copy the exact wording of a sales letter you think is strong, in order to get a feel for the psychology, rhythm, style, and content of sales letters. Choose the letter from the ones you've collected. Copy the letter word-for-word as it appears. It's better to write in longhand rather than to type the letter because in this way you'll have a better understanding of the thought processes behind its overall construction.

    You may be thinking that this sounds like a lot of tedious work. It does take some time and effort to copy a sales letter in full. But I can personally vouch for this method of learning. What will it do for you? It will, in time, saturate your mind with the way sales letters are planned and written. Believe me.

- Montgomery Ward is pleased to announce a direct marketing opportunity that has never been offered before. (catalog advertising sales offer)

- Learn to Meditate Correctly, Easily and Naturally with an Expert in the Teaching Field! (headline promoting a meditation workshop)

- So many great things have been happening with our winners that we can confidently say that American Song Festival competitions are truly an "open door" to the music industry. (International songwriting competition)

- How would you like to be rich—starting almost immediately—without effort—without experience—without risk? (opening line from wealth-building system)

- Have you ever agonizingly pushed your legs from the warmth of a cozy bed on a cool morning and groaned to yourself, "Oh no, not another day"? (magazine subscription)

Step Two: Interest

The second step in the sales process is to arouse interest. Many letters accomplish this within a few paragraphs; other letters take a full page to do it. The point is do your best to get the prospect interested in your product or offer. And do it in just a few paragraphs.

How do you stimulate interest? By letting the reader of your sales letter know that what you have to offer is important, timely, helpful, profitable, or useful to him or her. Prospects want to know the benefits of your offer. Prospects will read the first paragraph and then decide whether to read more or tear up your letter. Yes. You'd be surprised how many sales letters get torn up and thrown in the wastebasket. So your goal is to whet the interest of your prospects so they'll want to read more. Self-identification is a powerful tool in arousing interest, and you should use it. If you can make the first few paragraphs relate to a prospect, and motivate the prospect to read on, you will have succeeded in arousing interest. I call this type of arousal the "you appeal." Through the "you appeal," you can prove to your prospect that it's worth his or her time to read more of your letter.

Here are several examples of opening paragraphs from effective sales letters. Notice how each one uses the "you appeal" and sums up the promise, benefit, and overall value of the product or offer. Here they are:

- From a sales letter offering a way to make money:

  I'm sure you'll agree that the best job in the world would be one in which you work for yourself, set your own hours, live anywhere you wish, and see your income rise or double year after year. IT COULD ALL BE YOURS!

- From a sales letter offering a report on how to get more out of life through walking:

  Once Your Legs Go, Can the Rest Be Far Behind?

  Got the tummy ache, backache, headache, the blues, that tired run-down feeling? Whatever it is that may be ailing you, walking will make you feel better.

- From a sales letter offering a system for creating new ideas:

  If you would like to increase your income each and every year—and have a wonderful time doing it by creating your own original ideas—then let me explain how I learned to do it.

Whenever you sit down to plan and write a new sales letter, keep the following advice in a place where you can see it at all times: Your sales letter is received by an *individual*. You may send out thousands of letters, but each one will be read by an individual.

Popular radio and television personality Arthur Godfrey built a brilliant broadcasting career through his ability to make each member of a large audience feel and believe that commercial messages are directed only to themselves. He spoke and communicated to each listener as an individual. This me-to-you feeling was a major reason for his huge success.

Step Three: Conviction

The third step in the sales process is conviction. You must convince a prospect that what you're offering has real value and is worth the price you're asking. Your goal in this step is to make prospects see themselves using and benefiting from your offer now—not some time in the future. Creating an image in the mind of a prospect is a way to instill this conviction. Try to use words and sentences that will create pictures in a prospect's mind. A good example of this is recreational vehicle sales. Salesmen sell these vehicles to prospects on a face-to-face basis. But think how the use of this type of item can create pictures in a prospect's mind. Remember. The human mind thinks in pictures. Superior selling, whether by mail or face to face, creates clear and attractive pictures in a prospect's mind. When prospects see themselves on the road traveling in style in a trailer and having the time of their lives, they will be strongly motivated to buy. So help prospects see themselves using your product or offer and benefiting from it in some way.

Another way to establish conviction is to get a prospect to agree to a series of points being made in your sales letter. It's psychologically hard for a prospect to think yes to a series of questions and then suddenly arrive at a no. Use points or questions that bring a yes response. Here is one example: "Wouldn't you like to bank more money each month, own your own part-time business, and be on the road to financial independence?" Try to phrase such questions in a fresh way, however, as many of them have been overused.

Many sales letters have a positive flavor. A lot of effective sales letters are written in a way that assumes a prospect can see the value of an offer and will buy it. This kind of positive impression in a sales letter is hard for many prospects to resist. A natural tendency in life is to think negatively. So receiving a sales letter just might be the most positive thing some people see all day. So try to saturate your sales letters with positivism and enthusiasm. The two go hand in hand and can work together to establish conviction. Once a prospect feels convinced about your offer, he or she is ready to be led to the last step of the sales process—the appeal for action.

Step Four: Action

The concluding step in the sales process is action. Every good ad has an appeal for buying action, and the same is true for a direct-mail sales letter. Getting attention, arousing interest, and establishing conviction are mostly wasted without a definite appeal for action. You want prospects to send you an order as soon as they finish reading your letter. So an appeal for action is a must.

Here are some examples of appeals for buying action taken from direct-mail sales letters. Some of the following appeals for action have proved to be highly successful:

> Please use the enclosed envelope now. (*subscription offer*)

> Now the choice is yours, throw this letter away and forget it as I once did, or prepare to embark on one of the most exciting adventures of your life. (*a system for building wealth*)

> We sincerely hope that you will read over the enclosed entry forms. IT COULD BE THE BREAK YOU'VE BEEN LOOKING FOR! (*The American Song Festival Competition*)

> The Circle of the Mystic and Occult Arts can open the door to this new life for you. I invite you to sign the Reservation Card and return it today. (*membership organization*)

> If you are interested, please let us know right away as our supply is pretty slim. Just verify that we have your correct name and address, and send the correct amount in cash or check for the number of reports you want. We'll send them promptly by return mail. (*report on family names*)

> If you are interested, please let me know right away as I have only ordered a small press run. You can order by using the coupon at the bottom of this page. (*report on government benefits*)

> Send for the book today. Remember, now more than ever you have a real money fight on your hands and it is only going to get worse. Here is a chance to put the odds on your side. (*book*)

A P.S. Adds Power

Be sure to add a P.S. at the end of your sales letter. Think of it as having a last word with someone who is reading your letter. A P.S. can influence powerfully potential customers to go ahead and send you an order. Some direct-mail experts claim that a sales letter with

most of my own letters. Here's the greeting for this example:

Dear Friend:

3. Attention-getting opening: Remember. The first few paragraphs determine whether a prospect reads on in your letter or not. Get the reader's attention fast. Here is the opening I'll use:

> If you would like to write and sell your own articles for *cash*, then let me explain how I learned to do it. And why I am so sure you can do it for profit too.

What do you think of this opening? Read it over again. It's short, to the point, and tells the reader at once what the offer is all about. The next step is to arouse the prospect's interest.

4. Section to arouse interest:

> I started writing 12 years ago. I thought of it at first as just a part-time hobby. But I soon fell in love with the writer's way of life.

> Six years ago, I made the decision to write full-time. I haven't been sorry. In fact, every day has been a new adventure.

> I haven't struck it rich yet as a writer. But I've made a very good living. And I've done it my way.

> If you like your work, the money usually takes care of itself. It's your life that counts the most—how you spend your days.

> I do all kinds of articles—from general interest material to profiles of famous people.

> The first year I went full-time I missed that regular paycheck. But I sold 50 articles. I was proud. And I knew I would do better.

> Last year I wrote and sold 200 articles. That's a lot of sales. But I know I can do even better. The future looks great.

You can make money as an article writer—just as I do—and have fun too. You can write when and where you want to and as much as you choose.

Article writing for profit can fit into the life you're now living.

You can write three articles a year or twenty or several hundred. You can write early in the morning or late at night. You're the boss.

Become an article writer and you will seldom be bored. You will get out in the world and talk to all kinds of people.

5. Section to establish conviction:

There are *eight* basic types of articles you can write. So you always have a variety of kinds of articles you can do.

It's a great life. Everything you do and everywhere you go can be possible subjects for articles from your pen or typewriter. When you're an article writer, you wake up in the morning enthused. Life is exciting. The whole world looks fascinating to an article writer.

My first published article 12 years ago brought me only $7.00. But seeing my article and name in print that first time was a big thrill. Something clicked inside me that day. I knew I would be an article writer for life.

I can help you write and sell your own articles for *cash*. In the 12 years I've been an article writer, I've sold thousands of articles and features to magazines and newspapers. I must be doing something right.

I've even had articles published in far off places like Hong Kong, England, Australia, New Zealand, Mexico, and South Africa.

When you become a selling article writer, THE ENTIRE WORLD is your market.

After 12 years of opening letters with checks in them for my articles, I still come running when I hear the postman arriving. Mail call is the HIGHLIGHT of my day.

AND I WANT THE SAME THING TO HAPPEN TO YOU. It can—and sooner than you think.

I've developed a system for writing and selling all kinds of articles. This report is based on my proven success as a professional. To get my system to you at the lowest possible cost, I've had it printed in easy-to-read report form on plain, white paper.

6. Section for appeal for buying action:

If you really want to write and sell your own articles for money part-time now—and maybe full-time later— then mail the order form to me today. I'll send you my report on writing articles for cash by return mail.

Then *you* decide if you want to order the additional materials I offer on how to specialize in certain article fields.

I *guarantee* your satisfaction with my article writing system or I will refund your money at once.

7. Closing: I'll use the close I like best and one that has worked well for me—"Best regards." You're free, of course, to use "sincerely," "very truly yours," or whatever you wish.

8. P.S.: Here is a good one for this report:

P.S. Today's mail alone brought me three checks for magazine articles, one newspaper feature acceptance, and four replies from editors expressing interest in new article ideas. Send the order form now and start *your own* writing success.

There you have it. A two-page letter has been created. There's no way of knowing how well this letter would sell unless it's printed and sent out as part of a direct-mail package to qualified prospects. But this letter is a good example of an actual sales letter written to sell a specific product via direct mail. Use it as a guide when doing your own sales letters. Notice that there are no long or wordy sections in this letter. Wordy letters are hard to read. Keep paragraphs short.

WILBUR ENTERPRISES
1765 Autumn Avenue
Memphis, Tennessee 38112

Dear Friend:

If you would like to write and sell your own articles for cash money, then let me explain how I learned to do it.

And why I am so sure you can do it too.

I started writing 12-years ago. I thought of it at first as just a part-time hobby. But I soon fell in love with the writer's way of life.

Three years ago, I made the decision to write full-time. I haven't been sorry. In fact, every day has been a new adventure.

I haven't struck it rich yet as a writer. But I've made a very good living. And I've done it my way.

Like the work that you're doing, and the money usually takes care of itself. It's your life that counts the most...how you spend your days. I write articles full-time. I do all kinds...from general interest articles to profiles of famous people.

The first year I went full-time I missed that regular pay-check. But I sold 50-articles. I was proud. And I knew I would do better.

Last year I wrote and sold 145-articles. That's a lot of sales. But I know I can do even better. The future looks better.

You can make money as an article writer..just as I do..and have fun too. You can write when and where you want to and as hard as you choose.

Article writing can fit into whatever life you're now living.

You can write three articles a year, twenty, or several hundred. You can write in the early morning or late at night. You're the boss! You will get out in the world and talk to all kinds of people.

Become an article writer and you will seldom be bored. You will get out in the world and talk to all kinds of people.

There are eight basic types of articles you can write. So you always have a variety of kinds of articles you can do.

It's a great life. Everything you do and everywhere you go can be possible subjects for articles from your pen. When you're an article writer, you wake up in the morning enthused. Life is exciting.

The whole world looks fascinating to an article writer.

My first published article 12-years ago brought me only $7.00. But seeing my first article and name in print that first time was a big thrill.

Something clicked inside me that day. I knew I was an article writer

for life.

I can help you write and sell your own articles for cash money. In the 12-years I've been an article writer, I've sold thousands of articles-features to magazines and newspapers. I must be doing something right.

I've even had articles published in far off places like Hong Kong, England, Australia, New Zealand, Mexico, and South Africa.

When you become a selling article writer, the entire world is your market.

After 12-years of opening letters with checks in them for my articles, I still come running when I hear the postman arriving. Mail-call is the highlight of my day.

And I want the same thing to happen to you. It can..sooner than you think.

I've developed a system for writing and selling all kinds of articles. This 6-part system is based on my proven success as a full-time professional.

To get my system to you at the lowest possible cost, I've had each part printed in easy-to-read form on plain white paper. If you like part one, you can order and go on to part 2 - 6.

You order each part of the system separately...one at a time..when you decide you want it. You move at your own speed this way.

If you really want to write and sell your own articles for money... part-time now and maybe full-time some day...then mail the order form to me today. I'll send you part one of my system by return mail.

Then you decide if you want to order part two. What could be fairer?

I guarantee your satisfaction with this system or I will refund your money at once.

Kindest regards,

L. Perry Wilbur

P.S. Today's mail alone brought me 3-checks for magazine articles, a newspaper feature acceptance, and 4-go-aheads from editors on new article ideas. Send the pink order form now for Part I and start your own writing success.

3 FREE EXTRAS! A free guide-sheet is sent with part one.
When you order part 3, free marketing for one of your articles is offered.
A free market report is offered when you order part 6.

* For still more proof, read over the enclosed blue insert.

A Two-page Sales Letter

The same goes for sentences—use simple ones. Avoid long or technical words. The easier and more appealing your sales letter is to read, the better the chances are that prospects will read all the way through the letter, be interested in your offer, and take buying action on the spot by sending you an order.

When you've written a sales letter that pulls, you'll certainly know it. The orders will flow in steadily or even in a flood. And that's when you'll know that all the planning and writing of your sales letter has been well worth it. You'll have a pulling sales letter, and that's the best kind.

THE ORDER FORM

The main thing to keep in mind about the order form in a direct-mail package is convenience. A carefully designed order form will make it easier for prospects to order from you and can save you money. One good way to save money on order forms is to have the form printed on one side of a sales letter. One of my sales letters has the order form printed on the bottom of one side so that prospects can detach the form and send it in the return envelope with their payment. This built-in order form has worked well for me.

If you decide to build the order form into your sales letter, be sure to leave enough space for the customer's name, address, city, state, country, and zip code. Have dotted lines printed after and between these entries to indicate where information is to be filled in. If the order form is printed on the same side of the paper as the sales message, have a dotted line printed on that side between the message copy and the form. This lets the customer know that this is the order form to be completed and separates it from the sales copy.

You might also wish to have a pair of scissors sketched in and shown clipping the order form along the dotted line. This can often influence the prospect to go ahead and send you an order. And request on the order form that the customer's name and address be printed. A printed name and address will save you the trouble of trying to figure out correct spellings. Customers often fill in the order form too quickly and will not print their names unless they are requested to do so.

At the top of my order form, I use the following statement to verify exactly what is being ordered: "Yes. Please send me my copy of *The Sure Way to Stop Smoking*. I understand that I will pay only

---

FREE TRIAL CERTIFICATE

WILBUR ENTERPRISES
1763 Autumn Avenue, Memphis, Tennessee 38112

My check or money order in the amount of $9.95 is
enclosed for the guide, Article Writing: The Best Job
in the World. I understand that I can examine the
guide for 7-days at your risk. If I decide to keep
the guide, I will owe nothing more. If I return it
within 7-days, you are to refund my $9.95.

▢ I'd like to see the first part of the guide...as
a sample...before ordering the rest of it. My check,
cash, or money order for $2 is enclosed.

Name (please print)

Address

City, State, Zip

Order Form

$6.95." A verification like this is a good idea because it makes ordering easier.

Below the customer's city, state, country, and zip code, many order forms have the words "check—cash—money order," with spaces after each. Customers then check which payment method they are using and send in the order.

Below the method of payment I usually indicate how the item will be mailed or shipped to the customer. So the last line of my order form reads: "Mailed via third-class mail. Please allow time for delivery. You may use this order form to send this item as a gift." It's a good idea to suggest to customers that the form can be used to send the product as a gift. Many mail-order customers will buy more than one item and send these items to friends or relatives as gifts. This is especially true around the Christmas season.

OTHER WAYS TO ORDER

Quite a few mail-order firms use a simple business reply card. The card can be postcard size or the size of a business envelope. I've seen a lot of reply cards, and the simple ones seem to work best. Many say something like this at the top: "Enroll Me Today," or "Mailing Order Label," or "This Offer Is Guaranteed." It's not necessary to say

lope—like the kind you see used for most business purposes. The smaller envelope is cheaper to obtain but not as businesslike. I use the long business reply envelope. In the upper left-hand corner I have three dotted-line spaces printed after the word "From." My company name and address is printed in the center of the envelope. For most of my offers I use black ink on white envelopes. A lot of mail-order operators claim that color envelopes usually outpull white ones. I suggest that you test both kinds, as I did.

How many reply envelopes you'll need depends on how much direct mail you plan to send out. I had several thousand envelopes printed when I first started my company and they were used up fast. You can also use reply envelopes when responding to requests for more details from the inquiry-and-follow-up ads you run.

Postage Stamps for Reply Envelopes

There are mixed feelings on whether a direct-mail user should supply the postage stamps for return envelopes. Many direct-mail operators claim that by providing stamps they can increase their orders received considerably; other operators feel the extra postage expense is not justified, and that prospects will use their own stamps if they really want to buy. You might wait until you're more established in your business before supplying return envelope stamps. Try mailing some envelopes with stamps and some without stamps to see what kind of results you get each way.

THE VISUAL EFFECT OF DIRECT MAIL

The use of color in direct mail can definitely increase the number of orders you receive. Prospects everywhere like and respond to colors. Using color means a higher printing expense, but the extra orders you receive make color worthwhile.

Color television sets have been around for some time. Have you ever watched a color television set for several weeks, and then switched to a plain black and white set? The contrast is strikingly evident. Millions of us everywhere have become used to color television; we take it for granted and certainly prefer it to black and white. This same effect of color is true in direct mail. Colors look inviting to the eye when prospects first open their direct-mail envelopes. A sales letter and circular are more appealing to read if printed in bright, attractive colors. This is not to say that you absolutely must use color in your direct-mail offers. You may not be able to afford the extra printing expense of color. Until you've gained some experience in direct mail, you may prefer to use black and white mailings. So keep the idea of using color in the back of your mind. As your business develops, sooner or later you'll want to use some color in your sales letters, circulars, and order forms.

It's, of course, true that the use of color is no guarantee that a particular product or offer of yours will do well. It's always the offer itself that counts. But the use of color does add an influence and visual stimulation to buy. When people glance through their mail, they're usually first attracted to color envelopes. A good example is the envelope sent out by the American Song Festival for its annual competition. The name and address of the festival appears in red, white, and blue on the upper left corner of the envelope. So a patriotic visual effect is achieved and it's appealing.

The mail-order departments of many book publishers use color effectively in their direct mailings. One publisher's sales letter I received is printed in black and green ink on white paper. It is very eye catching. Another letter of this type is printed in black ink on white paper, with key lines underlined in blue. The headline and closing of this letter is also blue.

Sales letters and business reply envelopes come in all styles and color combinations. One popular color combination used in sales letters is red and black ink on white paper—the effect is striking. The use of red ink in combination with other colors has become increasingly popular. One sales letter of mine printed in blue ink on white paper did particularly well. So it isn't always necessary to have two or three colors. It's well known in mail order that blue ink (and shades of blue paper) generally pull well with both male and female prospects. Men respond to blue somewhat better than women. Pink and canary yellow often bring a good response from women prospects. Your printer can suggest ideas and color schemes to create an unusual effect.

Many order forms use blue or green ink on a white background, or black ink on a gold background and are quite effective. An order form I've seen recently uses three colors. The order form is the exact size of a check and even looks like a check. The copy of the form is printed in black and red ink on a blue-green background. This is one of the best-looking order forms I've seen. This form will no doubt influence many prospects to send in an order.

Your First Use of Color

When you're ready to use color in your direct mailings, here are some color combinations to consider. These colors have worked well in my own business and also for many other mail-order operators. Here they are:

1. Blue ink on white paper
2. Blue and black ink on white paper
3. Red and black ink on white paper
4. Blue or black ink on canary-yellow paper
5. Black ink on pink paper (has strong appeal for women)
6. Black, green, and red in any combination of ink or paper

Black on White Can Pull Orders

Don't feel like you have to use color in your mailings to get orders. Color can often increase the response to your offers, but one of my first sales letters was printed in black ink on white paper and sold very well. Even if everything in your direct-mail package consists of black ink on white paper, it can still bring in orders. But if you can afford to use color, you should do so. Even one color—blue on white paper, for example, will bring you better results. Try sending out one mailing consisting of all black ink on white paper and another mailing using color, and then compare the results. This test may convince you that the extra expense for color is justified. But generally, most prospects are interested in your offer—not how much color is evident. So don't let the lack of color keep you from using direct mail.

Other Visual Effects

There are other kinds of visual effects used in direct mail. Some of them include the following:

1. Sketches and illustrations of the product or service in action.
2. Photographs of satisfied customers.
3. Photographs of the mail-order operators themselves used in a circular to influence prospects to buy.
4. Cartoon-type panels and balloons and humorous-looking figures using the product.

5. Occult or mystical-looking mazes, sketches, symbols, and designs used to sell occult products.

How to Use Visual Effects

A sound way to get visual effects into your mailings is to simply ask yourself how more visual effect can be applied to your direct-mail package. By keeping all of the visual possibilities in mind you're sure to come up with some good ideas. You don't have to be a commercial artist to add flavor and appeal to your mailings. You probably at least have the ability to draw a simple sketch showing your product in action. You can certainly draw stars, brackets, mystical circles, dollar signs, and other simple effects. Just keep thinking about what might make your letter come alive, liven up your circular, add appeal to your order form, and make the outside envelope more effective.

For my offer of a music guidance report, I used drawings of musical notes in my sales letter and circular. The notes added a lot of style to my offer and made my entire product stand out in the minds of prospects. You can come up with good visual effects like mine if you'll do some creative thinking. Keep asking yourself how your total package can be upgraded with some kind of visual effect. See what's being done in other direct mailings, and experiment with your own ideas.

Visual effects can increase your direct-mail profits. Remember. The visual effects you use in your direct mailings can make your offers stand out from the competition. So use visual effects for extra selling power.

Part IV

PRACTICAL
CONSIDERATIONS

12
Filling Your Orders

ACKNOWLEDGING ORDERS

One aspect of running your mail-order business is acknowledging orders. There are two views on this. Some mail-order operators are convinced that sending acknowledgments to customers is a must for success. Other operators believe that sending acknowledgments is an extra expense and isn't necessary. The choice is up to you. But I urge you to choose carefully. If possible, it's better to send an acknowledgment. But there will be days when you are busy and you will forget to send acknowledgments. I usually send acknowledgments, but I have neglected to send them at times. If you are in mail order on a part-time basis, you may not always have enough time to send acknowledgments.

Sound Reasons for Sending Acknowledgments

Here are some sound reasons for mailing an acknowledgment back to a customer as soon as possible:

1. It's good business. It instills good will and confidence in the customer for you and your company.
2. It makes a customer feel that he or she is important and valuable to your company.
3. It shows your appreciation for a customer's order.

4. It encourages repeat business.

5. It stimulates customer loyalty.

6. It assures customers that their orders have arrived safely.

Remember. An acknowledgment is your written confirmation to a customer that his or her order has been received. People often worry about their mail being lost. Acknowledgments do a lot to erase this worry and help to upgrade the reputation of the mail-order industry. Therefore, acknowledgments are worth the extra time and money and can aid you in building a successful mail-order company.

Types of Acknowledgments

There are two types of acknowledgments—the form and the personal letter. Both types state that the order has been received and will be filled as quickly as possible. Many mail-order operators prefer the personal letter type of acknowledgment because it has warmth and shows a greater feeling of appreciation to the customer. Sending a form acknowledgment, however, is better than none at all. When you begin to receive hundreds of orders daily, you may be forced to use a form acknowledgment.

Many mail-order operators acknowledge all orders the same day they're received (within 24 hours). Mail-order firms that let orders sit around for days or weeks hurt the reputation of everyone in the mail-order industry. In the early stages of running your company, the question of whether to send acknowledgments may not seem very important. But this is the best time to start forming the habit of sending them to customers. In the long run, acknowledgments will increase your chances for a real and lasting success in mail order. Acknowledgments help to make every person who sends you an order a happy and satisfied customer. That's the kind of customer who will keep your business growing and prospering.

FILLING ORDERS PROMPTLY IS A MUST

You would think that all mail-order firms would automatically treat their orders with tender loving care. This just isn't true. There are many companies that react to orders with an uncaring and unprofessional attitude. Orders are the lifeblood of a mail-order business. Make it a rule now to handle orders with respect and efficiency.

One mail-order company advertises about the speed with which it fills orders. But customers have waited six to eight weeks to receive small orders from this company. Many mail-order printing firms take far too long to fill orders. In most of these cases, no explanation for the delay is given.

Why are orders treated so carelessly by some mail-order companies? One reason is the inefficiency of some employees today. They make errors. They misplace orders or let them accumulate unopened. At times, some of these companies only have a skeleton crew filling orders with little supervision. When you need help in your business, try to hire dependable people who will fill orders promptly.

Customers who have had bad experiences with mail-order firms often spread the word and sometimes contact postal authorities. Some mail-order companies have lost their right to do business by mail for delaying or not filling orders and for refusing to return a customer's money on a guaranteed offer.

Many people believe that service is a thing of the past. This is one reason why more and more people choose to do business by mail. So mail-order firms that fill orders carelessly hurt the firms that fill orders responsibly and professionally. Reputable mail-order companies fill their orders within 24 hours or a few days.

An Example of Poor Management

Some of the larger mail-order companies have poor service due to poor management. An order I sent to a mail-order printing company is a good example. I ordered 1,000 business reply envelopes and paid extra to have lines printed on the reverse side of the envelopes. I received this order, and later sent another order for the same kind of envelope. This time I received no order and got instead a note from the firm stating that they do not fill orders with printing on the reverse side of the envelope. I was amazed at this reply because the firm had filled the same order before. I wondered if some skeleton crew member had received my order, not felt like bothering with it, and sent me the note stating that my order couldn't be filled. What a way to do business. I never ordered from this firm again.

The Problem of Indifference

The average businessman used to take pride in seeing that all of his mail received a courteous, professional, and prompt reply. This is no longer true in many cases. As a test, I once sent a professionally typed letter on my business letterhead to 250 mail-order companies. A stamped return envelope was enclosed with half of the letters, but I received only 7 replies. This test is a good indication of how indifferent some mail-order companies have become. So as you build your own mail-order business, strive to answer all orders and requests in a careful, professional, and prompt manner. By doing this, you will build a solid reputation of integrity. And your mail-order company will grow and prosper.

KEEPING ACCURATE RECORDS

Keeping records in mail order is easy. The necessary records are simple and easy to maintain. When I launched my mail-order firm I got a three-ring notebook and some paper with twelve lines across it. This allowed me room for eight divisions (or headings) on each sheet of paper. I recommend that you do the same or use a similar system. I wrote the following headings across the top of each page:

Date Order Received
Name of Customer
Address of Customer
Amount Enclosed
Method of Payment
Date Order Filled
Postage Cost
Key Code

I found that eight columns to a page gave me enough room to record the essential information, but you might prefer to have only four divisions to a page. Let's take a look at each of these eight division headings.

Date Order Received

The date an order is received should be the first division in your record-keeping system. It's important to know the exact date on which you received an order or request for details. But when you receive a lot of orders, it's easy to forget to put down the dates they were received. I find that it's best to record the date of every order

Publication Ad Run in_____ Charge Per Word or Line_____

Address_____ Heading of Ad_____

Date Received	Name of Customer	Address of Customer	Amount Enclosed	Method of Payment	Date Order Filled	Key Code	Postage Cost

Record Keeping Chart

or inquiry received immediately after opening each day's mail. This way it gets done at once and before anything distracts you. But some mail-order operators put down the dates of orders received as the last business activity of the day. Either way is all right as long as you are sure to record each date. You'll find date information to be useful for income-tax purposes.

Name of Customer

The most vital information of all is the name of each customer who sends you an order for your product or service, or an inquiry request. When you record a customer's name in your records, write or type it just as you received it on the order form or envelope. Sometimes you can't be sure of the exact spelling of a customer's name because it is not written clearly. A good way to make sure that names are written legibly is to have customers print their names. Have a line printed on your order form requesting customers to "please print."

Many mail-order operators also type or print the names of their customers on index cards. Remember. These names are valuable to you. Don't lose them. Each index card is a record of your business with a customer. Each offer that a customer buys and the date the order was received should be listed on the index cards. Whether the customer responded directly from an ad, sent in an inquiry, or replied to your direct-mail package should also be listed. I know this sounds like a lot of record keeping, but I cannot stress enough how important this information is to you. It's as good as money in the bank, for it will enable you to sell to customers repeatedly. And, also, your list of names can be sold to other mail-order operators.

Address of Customer

You should write down the address of each customer on your record sheet and also on your index card. By having the addresses written down in two separate places, you will be less likely to lose them. Many mail-order customers have a post office box in their address, so be sure to record the numbers correctly. Double-check each address, and don't forget to include zip codes. Zip codes usually speed up the delivery of your mail.

Amount Enclosed

"Amount enclosed" is that lovely looking column on your record sheet where you record the amount of money sent in by each customer. My record sheets show long columns of money sent to me ranging from $0.50 to over $20.00. The average amount I've received since I began my mail-order business is $10.00

When you begin to receive your first orders with cash, checks, and money orders in them, the full scope of this amazing mail-order business will begin to dawn on you. Even if your first offers are low-priced items, it will be exciting just to open your mail and find money inside. Once this happens, I predict that it would be hard to get you out of mail order.

For inquiries received (for more details on your offers), you can simply write "inquiry" in the column used for the amount enclosed. Or you can have a separate column on your record sheet headed "Inquiries." This way, each time you receive an inquiry on an offer from a customer, just put a check mark in the inquiry column for that customer's name. This is the way that I record inquiries.

Method of Payment

Did your customer send you cash, check, or money order? You record this information in the "Method of Payment" column. By referring to this column, at any time in the future you can see how offers were paid for.

I advise against using C.O.D. orders because special postal arrangements must be made and it's not as popular a payment method today as it has been in the past. Once your business has grown larger, you might want to use C.O.D., but most customers prefer cash, check, or money order.

Date Order Filled

The date you mail your product or details on an offer is recorded in the "Date Order Filled" column. This information is important because it verifies that each order has been mailed.

Postage Cost

The amount of money you spend on postage is recorded in the "Postage Cost" column. You definitely need to keep up with how much money you spend on postage. Postage costs can add up quickly—especially when you're filling hundreds of orders each month.

Key Code

The last column heading on your record sheet should be the key codes. This column will let you know which ads are pulling in the most orders. When the same key keeps appearing in this column, you'll know that the ad it represents is definitely a winner.

This eight-column system is a simple way of keeping records for your mail-order business. You might want to alter this system by using an entire sheet of paper, a special form, or a file folder for each heading. There are, of course, more elaborate systems you could use. In time, you may develop your own form of record-keeping system. But the eight-column system will get you started. It has worked well for me and it can work for you.

Other Business Expenses

A good place to keep a record of your other business expenses is on your record sheets in a separate section of your three-ring notebook. The following are examples of column headings for other expenses.

- Date Expense Incurred
- Description
- Advertising Expense
- Printing Expense
- Professional Service Expense

The point is to keep up with your expenses in a way that does not confuse you. Any method that is logical and businesslike is okay. The records you maintain are tangible proof of the money you spend on your business. This can be very important when income-tax time rolls around.

13

Mail-Order Fraud

FALSE ADVERTISING HURTS HONEST ADVERTISING

The sad thing about mail-order fraud is that it hurts the honest people in the industry who are offering legitimate products with genuine value. After being cheated once, victims of swindlers may never trust another ad or piece of direct mail they receive. Mail order would be an even richer and larger industry today if all those who've been cheated could be brought back into the buying-by-mail fold.

Along with the majority of honest and enterprising men and women who are attracted to mail-order, con artists and swindlers have also found a home. Like other industries, there are a number of bad apples in mail order. In the United States alone, over 142,000 complaints for mail fraud were received by the Postal Service last year. And the number of complaints continues to rise. The following are the main reasons for these complaints:

1. Orders that are never received.
2. Orders that are halfway filled but never completed.
3. Orders that arrive in damaged condition.
4. Orders that arrive safely but don't work as advertised and are unsatisfactory.
5. Requests for money-back refunds that are not honored.

Research conducted by the Federal Trade Commission reveals that over 6,000 companies in the United States do more than $40 billion a year in mail-order sales. And this figure is increasing each year. In the words of Jerome Lamet, the assistant regional commissioner of the FTC's Chicago office, "There isn't a day that goes by that we don't get one or two complaints about mail-order companies."

A man in Illinois was arrested recently for cheating customers out of $2 million. His product was a $16.95 digital watch, and the ad for it promised a free pocket calculator for every order of two watches. The catch is that nobody ever received a watch, even though thousands of people sent in cash orders. Not one watch or calculator was ever received. Finally, postal authorities stopped all mail to the company. A whopping $1.2 million of the money was eventually traced to various banks. Another $800,000 was stashed in Mexican banks and may never be recovered.

According to postal inspectors, Americans lost $514 million to mail-order fraud in a recent year, and this figure is $119 million more than the year before. False advertising and misrepresented products are filling the bank accounts of swindlers, con artists, and crooks. Beware of "pie-in-the-sky" promises and "riches-beyond-your-wildest-dream" deals.

Some Victims Are Veterans

One mail-order firm sent direct-mail offers to veterans that looked like government notices. Many veterans know that they have some form of burial benefits, but they don't know exactly what they are. So when they read this direct-mail offer concerning burial benefits, they thought it was part of a government program. And, consequently, many veterans lost money because of this scheme.

LAND FRAUD

Land sale is a big mail-order business. You'd be surprised how much land is sold by ads and direct mail. Many land sales are entirely ethical and genuine. But a lot of land—entirely worthless—is sold to gullible buyers.

The advertising used in crooked land deals is very misleading, if not false. Many people buy land sight unseen, and that's where the swindle comes in. The direct-mail sales brochure that prospects see describes the land site in beautiful color pictures and exciting copy.

There are usually mountains in the near background. A town is also near the land. But when mail-order buyers visit the land they've bought, they often discover that the mountains aren't as close to their land as the pictures indicated, the town is further from their land than advertised, there are few roads to and from their land, and the true value of their land is much less than what they had been led to believe. People from all walks of life have sunk thousands of dollars into half- or full-acre ranchettes, and later find out that the real estate they've bought is almost worthless. Retired people are prime targets for crooked and fraudulent land deals.

One way mail-order land development firms spark the initial interest of prospects is through a free dinner, film, and trip to the land site. I once received an invitation in the mail to a free steak dinner and color-film showing of New Mexico land a company was offering. I accepted. I had a fine meal that didn't cost me a cent, watched a very interesting film about the state of New Mexico, and came close to flying out to the land site. A free dinner and film is a strong way of stimulating interest in a land offer. Some land offers presented in this way are genuine and conducted by ethical companies.

A HUD Warning on Land Deals

A bulletin issued by HUD (United States Department of Housing and Urban Development) warns people about mail-order land deals: "A development might be described as 10 miles from Rainbow City without any indication that the 10 miles leads through an impassable swamp and that it is 34 miles via passable roads."

Another misleading ad offers buyers a chance to become a "land baron" for just a few dollars down and $20 a month. These potential buyers imagine that they can own a big chunk of land, but the actual dimensions turn out to be more like 50 by 140 feet.

CHAIN LETTERS

There's been a sharp increase in the number and variety of chain letters in the last few years. But the word is out on chain letters. Postal authorities say that "any chain letter which seeks something of value may be a violation of the federal lottery or mail fraud statutes." If a chain letter seeks to circulate things of no value—such as a recipe—it is entirely legal. Some chain letters are able to operate on the fringe of the law and, even though they are rip-offs, are considered legal. Most chain letter schemes hurt the reputation of the mail-order industry.

A friend of mine once received a typical chain letter. The letter gave instructions on how to make a lot of money in a few weeks. My friend was advised to send $2.00 to the last name of five listed in the letter, type his own name as the first name on the list, and omit the last name on the list (the one he sent the $2.00 to). He was urged to have 200 to 500 copies of the letter printed and mailed to known mail-order buyers from a rented list. According to the letter, he could receive $10,000 or more by following these directions. So to prove to himself that sending out chain letters is a waste of time and money, he followed the instructions exactly. What was the result? A total zero. He never received one letter or dollar in the mail. There will probably always be gullible people who believe that they can get something for nothing. Don't fall for any of these chain letter schemes. Tear them up pronto whenever you receive one. Never become involved in any kind of chain scheme sent through the mail. It can tarnish your good name and reputation fast and could ruin your future in mail order. Treat your customers the same way you'd like to be treated. Even though you don't see your mail-order customers, you still have a responsibility to deal with them ethically and fairly.

OLD MAIL FRAUDS

People still seem to fall for the same old con deals. Some con deals are modernized or disguised in some way, but they still are rip-offs by mail. Here are several old con deals that are still being used today. Be on the alert for them.

1. Fake invoices for items that were never ordered.

2. Phony ads for products that are never shipped.

3. Phony work-at-home deals. Some of these are honest offers. But many buyers are cheated through an "easy money" approach.

4. Phony contests that hook "winners" into buying expensive products.

5. Pyramid schemes.

6. Nonexistent correspondence schools. Buyers are offered training for high paying and glamorous jobs that don't exist.

Check over this list when you are suspicious of an offer. Many con artists can be put out of business by reporting these crooked deals to your local postmaster. Most mail-order firms are honest and ethical, but the bad ones have to be eliminated.

George Davis, the assistant general counsel and head of the Postal Service's consumer protection office, says, "A lot of people have the attitude that if the ad is published, then they can trust the product. But we have no authority to check out a product in advance. We move in only when we get complaints about something." So to a surprising degree, the mail-order industry is a business of trust. Mail-order buyers trust that their orders will be shipped promptly and will arrive in good condition. A cash order, in itself, implies a buyer's trust in a mail-order firm.

A Phony Billing Scheme

Recently, postal inspectors discovered a phony billing operation. Seventy-five people were involved in the operation. A company, doing business as an advertising agency, sent bills to hundreds of consumers and businesses for advertising that they didn't do.

The Lure of Travel

Postal authorities consider an ad in a newspaper to be use of the mail. One way that many unemployed teenagers in large cities are being cheated is through the lure of travel. Teens are hooked through "travel the world—all expenses paid" ads. What this "travel" turns out to be is the door-to-door selling of books, magazines, and other products in far away places. The pay is commission, and the "expenses paid" is a draw against the commission. These ads are misleading, but teenagers looking for work continue to fall for them. Some of the same frauds are still being used today. As long as there is mail service in countries around the globe, there will probably be mail fraud.

NEW MAIL-ORDER REGULATIONS

Since the FTC has laid down new mail-order regulations, there have been fewer complaints about mail order firms not sending goods that have been ordered and paid for. Some of these new rules require mail-order firms to do the following:

1. Inform every customer within 30 days that their order has been received.

2. Supply customers with a postage-free way to cancel a delayed order (a reply card, for example).

3. Refund a customer's money within 7 business days after receiving a notice of cancellation.

The FTC now has the power to take mail-order companies that violate these laws into court. An injunction can be obtained against any mail-order firm in violation of the regulations. The present penalties for violations range up to $10,000 per day.

14

Mail-Order Millionaires

Through the rest of this century and beyond, prosperous growth is predicted for the mail-order industry. Mail-order profits can be enormous, and you have just as good a chance to get your share of them as anyone else. Over the years, mail-order operators have done well—part-time and full-time. Many have become mail-order millionaires. I have no way of knowing how well you will do in mail order. But I can assure you that the day you launch your mail-order company, you'll be entering a fabulous growth industry. The chance to make more money than you ever dreamed is waiting for you in mail order.

MANY MAIL-ORDER MILLIONAIRES STILL ADVERTISE

Read the leading mail-order publications, and you'll notice that many millionaires still run classified ads. There's a four-star lesson here. Why do individuals who have become millionaires via mail order continue to run classified ads? Because they learned long ago that classified ads will continue to build their invaluable customer list. Most mail-order millionaires owe a lot of their success to classified inquiry and follow-up ads. These ads helped to get their business off the ground and continued to help through the years. So these established mail-order millionaires still run small classified ads regularly. This does make a strong case for you to use classified ads. If small classified ads worked well for many mail-order millionaires, these ads should work for you.

MAIL-ORDER SUCCESS STORIES

Remember. The mail-order millionaires of today were once new-comers to mail order. They wondered how they might start and build a profitable mail-order company of their own. They thought about which items would be best to offer by mail. They planned their classified ads and direct-mail offers carefully. They tested new ideas and found the right offers. And they kept on plugging. When one offer proved to be a dud, these operators didn't give up. They went back to the drawing board to find something else that would work. Let's take a look at some of these self-made millionaires of mail order.

John D. MacArthur

John D. MacArthur saw opportunity in mail order. He became fabulously wealthy by parlaying a $2,500 mail-order insurance firm into a vast fortune. He was said to be worth $5 billion when he died in 1978.

The son of a Pennsylvania minister, MacArthur went to work for a Chicago insurance firm owned by his brother Alfred when he was eighteen. He later tried newspaper work but didn't care for it. After a stint with the Royal Canadian Flying Corps during World War I, he returned to the insurance business. With a loan of $2,500, MacArthur bought Bankers Life Insurance Company. This was at the time of the Great Depression, and it was difficult to get good quality salesmen. So he decided to try selling insurance by mail. This was the smartest move of MacArthur's career. His company prospered. Mail orders for insurance with Bankers Life came in continually. Before long, Mac-Arthur was buying out other companies.

Here's something to remember about MacArthur. He kept his cool when he first started to make money: "I didn't want to change my lifestyle because I was afraid something might happen. I was on thin ice for the first 15 years." Many newcomers to mail order fold up their companies after their first year of business because of low profits. This attitude shows a lack of purpose and planning. Some companies do make a lot of money the first year. Many others don't. The point is that many fortunes in mail order were built over many years. And in most cases, the first several years were uncertain and difficult.

E. Joseph Cossman

Another mail-order success story is that of E. Joseph Cossman. This ingenious man made his fortune largely from showing others how to build wealth. But Cossman has a profitable organization called the Future Millionaires Club and many other enterprises—all money-makers. He is proof that you don't have to put all your eggs in one basket.

Cossman's key purpose now is "to help others realize the dream that I had come true for myself. The whole secret is in sales—the market of supply and demand. It's there for anyone with initiative and know-how who wants to get it."

100,000 NEW MILLIONAIRES

Here's an astounding fact to ponder. The Internal Revenue Service (and they should know) recently predicted that 100,000 new millionaires will emerge within the next two years in the United States. According to Robert Schwartz, 10,000 of these new tycoons will be "counterculture millionaires." Schwartz runs a school for promoters and cites these books as examples of profitable counterculture products: *The Whole Earth Catalog, Zen and the Art of Motorcycle Maintenance,* and *The Inner Game of Tennis.* All three earned fortunes. Schwartz believes strongly that millions of people will pay well for products and services that will enrich their lives. Schwartz thinks that many new counterculture millionaires will make their fortunes almost without trying: "What motivates them is mainly an interest in achievement. Such an entrepreneur is first of all a missionary with a zeal about a new vision."

MAKING YOUR FIRST MILLION

To many people making a million dollars seems impossible. But one of the first musts for becoming a millionaire is believing that it's possible to become a millionaire. So here are some rules to help you on your way to becoming a mail-order millionaire.

1. Devise a plan for your future. The character of Luke in the film *Cool Hand Luke* said that he never had a plan or knew what he was going to do next. Maybe that's why his life added up to nothing. If you have a plan, write it down. Add to it and

rewrite it if necessary. Perfect and improve it as best you can. Study it often.

2. Be realistic. Realize that there are obstacles in your path to success. Decide how they can be overcome or removed.

3. Increase your self-discipline.

4. Don't join a large corporation. The odds are great that you'll get lost in the corporate shuffle. If often takes many years to move up to the top positions in big companies. Your chances are better with a younger and smaller company with growth potential.

5. Use your free time wisely. Many people have become millionaires by devoting most of their time to their careers. Many millionaires are strongly motivated people who turned a hobby into a profitable business. These people never get discouraged even though they often put in 75 to 100 hours a week.

6. Rely on yourself. Depending on others can be frustrating and a disaster at times. A good example of self-reliance is Irving Thalberg, the legendary Hollywood producer during the Golden Age of films. Thalberg ruled over Hollywood like a prince in the 1920s and 1930s. His long period of illness as a youth gave him time to think about his future. In making his plans for a business career, he devised his own rules that he would live by: "Never take any one man's opinion as final. Never think your own opinion is unassailable. Never expect help from anyone but yourself."

7. Think positive about your work, the future, and life itself. There really is power in positive thinking. It's been proven many times.

8. Do it now. This was the success formula of W. Clement Stone, Chicago insurance tycoon and multimillionaire. It helped him to build his own enormously successful company—Combined Insurance Company. Success does not come to one who waits. Always have a list of things to get done for every day. After you get the big things accomplished for each day, you can then turn your attention to the less important things. This is one of the most effective ways to get more done. Many top executives practice it consistently.

9. Develop your imagination. Imagination is a priceless creative ability. Walt Disney, Grandma Moses, Cole Porter, and Will Rogers became successful through imagination. Imagination can be especially helpful in mail order. Try to imagine what new inventions, services, and scientific advancements the future will bring.

THE FUTURE OF ADVERTISING

Advertising is a growth industry. And as an operator of your own mail-order firm, you're part of this industry. Last year, $37 billion was spent on advertising, and this figure is expected to be 15 percent higher this year. Advertising will be a boom industry for the rest of this century and beyond. So learning how to advertise your mail-order products and services is worthwhile. There's a growing need for more informative, interesting, and effective advertising.

THE WILLINGNESS TO TRY SOMETHING NEW

Trying something new can be the way to a fortune. It takes faith in yourself, but the payoff can be fabulous. Walt Disney's dream of an amusement park for children, built around his cartoon and film characters, eventually became Disneyland and Walt Disney World. How about the McDonald's fast-food success story? It was all started by Ray Kroc, a man who believed in a new idea.

Many editors told DeWitt Wallace in the early 1920s that his idea for a magazine that would publish condensed versions of major articles was unworkable. But Wallace knew it would work. His idea became a reality in the form of the *Reader's Digest*.

EXTRA MONEY IN YOUR CUSTOMER LIST

Remember, your customer list is another source of profit and income for your mail-order business. You can rent your list to other mail-order dealers, insurance firms, correspondence schools, publishers, and corporations. You can sell your list of names, but you'll only get one flat payment and nothing else. By renting your list, you will have a constant income source. A big list company like Dunhill can offer your list to literally thousands of businesses. So when you get enough customers to make it worthwhile, you can increase your income by renting your name list to professional list firms.

FACTS FOR YOUR MAIL-ORDER FUTURE

Here are some facts about Americans—compiled by the Census Bureau—that can be useful in planning your future in mail order:

1. Life expectancy is increasing. A girl born today is expected to live to her late 70s.

2. Nine out of ten people are satisfied with their family life. But three out of ten want divorce actions made easier to obtain.

3. The divorce rate is increasing. It has more than doubled since the 1950s. There are now three times as many children associated with divorce as there were 20 years ago.

4. The most popular type of outdoor entertainment is horseracing. It presently draws over 60 million fans—about double the number of fans who watch baseball, which is in second place. Greyhound racing comes in third, with professional football and basketball in fourth and fifth positions.

5. Television is the favorite pastime of three out of ten people.

6. Americans are better educated now than at any other previous time in history. But they lack practical knowledge. Twenty percent of adults are functional illiterates.

7. The crime rate is skyrocketing. Crimes against people and property have tripled in less than 20 years.

8. The average family size is declining. It is presently 3.4 members. By 1990, the average married couple will have only one child.

Remember. You may never become a millionaire by running a mail-order company, but the opportunity always exists. Having your own business and seeing it continue to prosper year after year is always exciting. And the chance to one day hit the mail-order jackpot is a continuous challenge.

15

The Sure Way to Mail-Order Profits

Mail-order is interesting, challenging, and rewarding. It's very satisfying to create a brand new product or service of your own, advertise it, and then build it into a consistent winner.

John D. Rockefeller once offered some excellent advice: "When you hear about a good thing, don't delay. Get in while you can." Mail order is a good thing. And you should do well in it. But there are pitfalls to avoid, and you'll soon find that mail order is a business in which common sense can pay off in cold, hard cash.

MAIL ORDER IS A BUSINESS OF IDEAS

Remember. Mail order is a business of ideas. You need ideas for products and services. You'll also use ideas to advertise these offers. I want you to think about three dynamic ideas. Each one has earned a fortune. The paper clip is the first one. It's been around for a long time and is always useful—but think about how simple it is. The second idea is the game of Monopoly. It's still the best-selling game ever made. Think of the pleasure it has brought to people everywhere. Think of how Monopoly offers each player a chance to be a rich property owner for a while—even though it's only a game. Think of the wide appeal this fascinating game has. The third idea is the hula hoop. It may have been a fad, but it made its originator wealthy. It caught the imagination of the public and sold like mad. The public—young and old alike—just couldn't resist buying the hula hoop and trying it out. It was a real winner. Now here's the point. Blockbuster ideas can make you rich. And sometimes all you need is one good idea. How do you know you can't think of a profitable product idea until you try? You have just as much chance as anyone else to come up with a great idea for a mail-order product.

MAIL ORDER IS A BUSINESS OF PRODUCTS

Remember that mail order is also a business of products. So start thinking now about products. Saturate your mind with old products, new products, any products. Time spent thinking about products is never wasted. Research old products. Look at mail-order publications of 20 or 30 years ago. What was selling well then? Sometimes bringing back an old product is highly profitable.

Believe me. You never know when a new product idea may be forming in your mind. And this idea could develop into a blockbuster and make a fortune. Here are some important characteristics to consider when you have a mail-order product in mind. Use the following list as a guide when you compare your product to competing products.

1. Price
2. Size and weight
3. Versatility
4. Appearance and style
5. Performance
6. Durability
7. Accuracy or speed
8. Convenience
9. Installation cost

YOUR PROJECTED SALES VOLUME

There's power in expectation. So you should set sales volume goals for your mail-order business. When you start your mail-order company, ask yourself what your sales volume should be for your first six months or year in business. Here is a good way to record these sales goals.

First Year	First Product	Second Product	Total Sales
	$ _____	$ _____	$ _____
Units	_____	_____	_____
Second Year	$ _____	$ _____	$ _____
Units	_____	_____	_____

The following Small Business Administration booklets may be of help to you. They can be obtained from the Superintendent of Documents, Washington, D.C. 20402. At this time of writing, the booklets are free. Here are the titles:

- "What Is the Best Selling Price?" MA No. 193.
- "Marketing Planning Guidelines" MA No. 194.
- "Are Your Products and Channels Producing Sales?" MA No. 203.
- "Keep Pointed Toward Profit" MA No. 206.
- "Marketing Research Procedures" SBB9.
- "National Directories for Use in Marketing" SBB13.

THE ROAD TO MAIL-ORDER SUCCESS

As you proceed along the road to mail-order profits the following guidelines will help you. They will increase your profits, develop your confidence, and keep you moving ahead. Most of them have made a great difference in my own life. They can do the same for you. When used with the right mail-order products, these guidelines can lead you to substantial success.

1. Study—Continue to learn all you can about mail order There's always more to learn about this interesting and challenging industry.
2. Choose Your Offer Carefully—Again, much of the success of your business will depend on the quality of your products or

services. Choose them carefully. When one flops, try something else. Don't get discouraged if your first items do poorly. Thomas Edison tried 10,000 times before finding the right filament for the electric light.

3. Use Effective Advertising—Copy is king. Your job is to use the most effective form of advertising (classified ad, display ad, direct mail, or catalog) and to select the best copy. Choosing the best mail-order publications for your ads is also important.

4. Find Your Proper Rate of Growth—This will be determined by your own goals. Try to set a realistic objective for your first year in the business. You may decide to reach a certain level of growth and then remain at that point. It's up to you. But remember. Smaller goals once realized build confidence for achieving bigger goals. And real success doesn't come overnight.

5. Develop the Will to Win—Your own will, once aroused, developed, and well focused on your goals, is a powerful force. Margaret Mitchell, author of *Gone With the Wind*, spent 10 years of her life writing her novel. She said little about her work while creating it and was frequently kidded by friends for giving so much of her time to writing. But Margaret Mitchell knew what she wanted and she went ahead and wrote a successful novel. She was enormously talented, but talent alone—without willpower—isn't enough. Most great achievements have resulted from a strong combination of talent and will. You have the potential ability to attain real success in mail order: "Whatever the mind of man can conceive of can become a reality." Talent, ability, and knowledge are all important, but the human will can work wonders. Men have lifted cars in moments of crisis through the power of their own will. Most of us use only a small fraction of the power available to us through our own will.

6. Use Your Imagination—This is real magic. Use your imagination to think of one good product idea and it could make you rich. Set your first year goals, and use your imagination to reach them. Once you've developed your imagination, follow it. It will show you ways to move forward in your business. Be enthusiastic about your company, for enthusiasm fires the imagination.

A PROVEN GUIDE FOR SUCCESS

"Prince of Showmen" is what newspaper editors called P. T. Barnum. Also known as "The father of modern publicity methods and practices," "The Lord of Laughter and Fun," and "Dispenser of Amusement," Phineas Taylor Barnum believed in and followed a highly moral code of showmanship. His proven guide for success is still valid today and can increase your chances for success in mail order.

High on Barnum's list of steps for success is this practical pointer: "Select the vocation which is most congenial to your tastes." Millions of people dislike the work they do each day because they made a wrong vocational choice. Take stock of your own situation. If you're in the wrong kind of work, start making plans now to leave it. If you haven't entered the work force yet, you might think about starting your own mail-order company. Life goes by fast, so you should be doing the kind of work you like.

Let Money Work for You

"Let money work for you" is another Barnum suggestion for success. A growing savings account is money at work for you. It may come in handy when you least expect it to. "Every man needs a nest egg—a cash reserve," said Bernard Baruch, the great Wall Street financier. When an opportunity comes along, a cash reserve will enable you to take advantage of it.

Putting money to work can also mean investing it in a mail-order company of your own. Investing has paid off for a lot of people. Although Bob Hope, Steve Allen, and Gene Autry have earned a lot of money from their careers, a large part of their fortune was built through wise investments. The money you put into your mail-order company could turn out to be the best investment of your life.

Beware of the Horror of the Blues

Another tip on Barnum's guide for wealth and success is "not to let the horror of the blues take over you." Fight the blues with all your might, for they can wreck your plans and wipe out your enthusiasm. There's a definite way to send the blues packing every time. When a negative thought tries to take root in your mind, just pull it out. Allow only positive and constructive thoughts of success. Weed out the others. It takes a lot of mental discipline to keep negative thoughts out of your mind, but it's worth the effort.

Whatever You Do, Do It With All Your Might

"Whatever you do, do it with all your might" is the next Barnum pointer for success. If necessary, work at your goals day and night. Put your entire self into your projects, calling on all your powers to help you accomplish your aims. Be determined. There's tremendous power in a determined person; power that won't take no for an answer. If a profitable and successful mail-order business is what you want, get it! Don't give up on your goal. Make what you want a reality.

Ask yourself some key questions. Where would America be today if it had given up in 1776? What would the fate of the Union have been if Lincoln had given up his determination to preserve it? What would've happened to England if it had not taken a stand against Hitler? Remember. With determination, anything is possible.

Learn Something Useful

P. T. Barnum also believed very much in learning. "Learn something useful to fall back on" is one four-star suggestion on his guide to success. A variation of this is to have an alternate plan in case your original one doesn't work. Barnum himself, is a good example of learning something useful to fall back on. He had worked as a grocery store clerk after leaving grammar school, so the first thing Barnum did after moving to New York in 1834 was to open a grocery store. Eight years later, Barnum opened his own museum—The American Museum. Barnum had a natural ability as a promoter, but he had his grocery business to fall back on if necessary. Your knowledge of mail order could prove to be the "something useful" you have to fall back on.

Another example of this idea for success is Thomas Jefferson. He had a great desire to learn something useful all his life. He spent five years to prepare himself for law, but he didn't limit his study to that field alone. He wanted a wider background of knowledge and knew that it would make him a better lawyer. So besides law, Jefferson studied political science, philosophy, Spanish, Italian, German, and some American Indian languages. Through the years, he learned many useful things that helped him to become a lawyer, statesman, scientist, architect, farmer, inventor, and musician. If Jefferson's career as a lawyer had ever floundered, he could've fallen back on the other abilities and skills he had learned.

Barnum, however, would have been quick to emphasize that Jefferson was a rare kind of genius. Few individuals can become masters of so many interests. So Barnum added this warning to his code for success: "Give the business you're in enough time."

Who knows what the coming years will bring! The time to prepare for tomorrow is today. The money, time, and effort you spend on mail order today may mean a great deal to you in the future.

Don't Scatter Your Powers

Barnum voiced a warning in this way: "Do not scatter your powers—stick to one kind of business only—until you succeed or experience shows you must abandon it." Barnum believed strongly that a fortune can slip through your fingers if you are working in too many occupations at one time. But Barnum, a genius in his own right, defied his own warning here, as he found time to run for Congress, to write his autobiography, to serve as mayor, and to open his own circus.

Depend on Your Own Personal Exertions

"Exercising both caution and boldness, depend on your own personal exertions," advised P. T. Barnum. At 19, Barnum founded and edited a newspaper in Danbury, Connecticut through his own personal efforts. Most worthy accomplishments and achievements depend on personal exertions. Students who earn academic degrees learn this early. They know they have to stay in there and keep plugging away at the books to get their degrees. One college professor, in summing up the trials and tribulations of getting a PhD, said it was like jumping through flaming hoops. He just kept jumping through them until he got his degree. Depending on your own personal exertions can pay off in many ways.

Be Systematic

Still another direction of the Barnum success guide is "to be systematic and to have the time and place for everything." Even the Bible backs this up and states that "there is a time for everything—a time to live, a time to work, a time to die." To keep advancing toward the success you seek, each night list—in order of their importance—the things you must do the next day. Then do these things. Planning your work and working your plan is a system that always works if you stick to it.

P. T. Barnum

Advertise Your Business

This is, of course, automatic for someone entering the mail-order field. Barnum felt that "advertising your business is a must." If you don't sing the praises and qualities of your business, who will? If Barnum believed in advertising in the 1870s, you can see how vital it is today.

When Barnum realized that his own name was a big factor in his success, he fully exploited his name. He's been compared to Shakespeare for his advertising genius and eloquence. When word spread that P. T. Barnum would be present for a circus performance, the box office take was always higher. Many people were just as interested in seeing the prince of showmen as his circus. But remember. Although Barnum was the author of statements like "there's a sucker born every minute," he drew a sharp line between innocent humbug and fraud.

Read the Newspapers

A final must for success, according to Barnum, is to "read the newspapers." Barnum evidently learned that the New York museum was for sale by reading a newspaper. Opening his American Museum was an important step in his career. "All I know is what I read in the papers," said Will Rogers. Ideas that have led many to success and riches have come from reading newspapers regularly.

Barnum's Success System Works

Phineas T. Barnum practiced his own success rules, including one he listed as "preserving your integrity." He liked his notoriety, but he always gave the public more than it paid for, and he made sure that his shows were in good taste. He firmly believed that the public deserved wholesome amusement.

There you have it. The personal success guide of P. T. Barnum, perhaps the greatest showman and promoter of all time. Barnum practiced what he thought daily and was widely known and loved for his sunny, alive nature; his constant desire to make people happy; and the improvement he brought to every town in which he lived. In the eyes of the public, he was a living Horatio Alger hero. When he died in 1891, his last words were a request to know the circus receipts for the day. Barnum was worth $5 million when he died. That was quite a fortune for that time. He was rich not only in money but also in friends, family, and a sense of worthwhile accomplishment.

As you plan your success in mail order keep Barnum's guide in mind. His ideas are well worth following today. Mail order is advertising and promotion. And P. T. Barnum was a brilliant promoter and advertising genius. Barnum's guide to success has helped me to make money in mail order and to become a widely published writer, copywriter, songwriter, college teacher, public speaker, winner of national awards, and advertising consultant. So refer to his words of wisdom often and try to apply his proven guide for success in your own life and mail-order business. Here are the ten points of Barnum's guide for success:

1. Select the vocation which is most congenial to your tastes.
2. Let money work for you.
3. Beware of the horror of the blues.
4. Whatever you do, do it with all your might.

5. Learn something useful.

6. Don't scatter your powers.

7. Depend on your own personal exertions.

8. Be systematic.

9. Advertise your business.

10. Read the newspapers.

The Magic of a Fresh Start

Nothing helps a person more in life than to make a fresh start. You may have tried to find your place in other industries without much success. If so, then a mail-order business of your own could be just the fresh start you need. Perhaps launching a mail-order company will be your first experience in the world of business. Whatever your situation may be, the freshness and stimulation of a new start can work wonders in your life. But for every person who dares to make a fresh start, millions of people are afraid to take the plunge and don't realize that what they need in their humdrum lives is new enthusiasm. A mail-order business can provide this enthusiasm.

WELCOME TO THE WORLD OF MAIL ORDER

Use this book to make your start in mail order, and refer to it often. I know that you can be a part of the exciting future of mail order. Whether you stick with a few products or grow into a giant business, a lot of satisfaction and personal fulfillment awaits you in this business. Maybe one of your products or services will improve the lives of your customers. It's a nice feeling to know that you've made a contribution to the lives of others and to the world in which you live. Bernard Baruch said it well: "The future is actually bright with promise. The trend of civilization itself is always upward." Welcome to the mail-order business. May your products be consistent winners, your ads pull stacks of orders, and your profits make all your dreams come true. See you in the fascinating world of mail order.

appendix I

Checklist for Success in Mail Order

1.   Remember that mail order is an item business.

2.   Use short and attractive headlines to hook prospects into reading your classified ads.

3.   Try to acknowledge every order you receive. It's good business.

4.   Consider offering a self-improvement booklet—their sales have skyrocketed recently.

5.   Be sure to use a professional-looking letterhead for all of your business correspondence. And type your letters.

6.   Avoid pie-in-the-sky copy in your ads offering unbelievable promises or overnight riches. Don't try to fool prospects. Offer genuine value for their money.

7.   Watch for important trends in the industry.

8.   Look over the "Window Shopping" mail-order section of *House Beautiful* magazine every month.

9.   Develop your creative and inventive abilities. This can lead to a jackpot.

10. Think about products or services you could offer to moon-lighters. There are 4,759,000 people in the U.S. holding down two jobs

11. Sell low-priced items directly from an ad for best results.

12. Guarantee your products and offers. You'll get more orders.

13. Avoid any offer that smacks of a chain letter or pyramid scheme.

14. Set a regular time for thinking up new product or service ideas for your business.

15. Offer a short manual on any subject—they often sell well.

16. Keep track of your growing customer list. An index card system is a good method.

17. Clip out classified and display ads that you feel are especially effective. Save them for future reference.

18. Consider offering a product to help people lose weight. There's a huge worldwide market for this item.

19. Allow for the rising postage rate in your direct mailings.

20. Make use of the "you appeal" in your ads.

21. Think of a way to prevent computers from being manipulated. Computer embezzlement is increasing weekly. Corporations will pay well for a computer theft prevention product or service.

22. Use inquiry and follow-up classified ads for higher-priced offers.

23. Think ahead. It will help you make more money in mail order.

24. Don't use a catalog to sell your offers until your customer list has at least 10,000 names.

25. Remember the dominant wants of people. Try to offer items that include many of them.

26. Always enclose a reply envelope—preferably a postpaid one.

27. Know that $100 spent on a direct mailing to 1,000 names should return you $300 or more. Anything less is not profitable enough. Higher postage rates will call for adjustment of these figures in the years ahead.

28. Before you offer a new product or service, decide who your customers are and the best form of advertising to reach them.

29. Know that you're bound to find a winner sooner or later.

30. Keep new ideas cooking on the back burner of your mind. The safety razor with its removable blade made its originator a millionaire.

31. Be sure to appeal for action by asking prospects to send you an order.

32. Offer some kind of a pet product by mail.

33. Use headlines printed in black and red colors on the outside envelope (the envelope received by prospects)—this is quite effective.

34. Keep your eyes and ears open for profitable new business ideas.

35. Handle any complaints immediately. Respond with a courteous letter of explanation.

36. Think about what kind of information, instruction, or special sounds you could put on record or tape and sell by mail.

37. Use the extra incentive of a free bonus gift. It's a proven way to increase your orders.

38. Try new selling strategies and concepts. Experiment by changing the headlines, copy, and size of your ads.

39. Use a short, easy-to-remember name for your mail-order company.

40. Advertise consistently—it's the way to make money in mail order.

41. Offer a product that cannot be bought in retail stores—a money belt is a good example.

42. Be sure to use a P.S. at the end of your direct-mail sales letter. It gives your offer extra pulling power.

43. Use a post office box so you can pick up your mail when you want it. The rental fee is small.

44. Know that the wife of the family of the future will be even more of a full partner and breadwinner.

45. Realize that a person's richest accomplishments may take place at any time from age 20 and beyond.

46. Work first with manufacturers in your own area or nearby when you use a drop-ship arrangement.

47. Remember that the names you receive from requests for details on your offers can grow into a profitable mailing list.

48. Offer a correspondence course. Many of the home-study firms in the United States are operated by individuals.

49. Write the copy for your ads with the mass audience in mind.

50. Look for items that serve the people of today. Smart mail-order operators change with the times.

51. Watch the ads in leading mail-order publications. Request details yourself, so you can look over current offers and literature used to sell them.

52. Don't start a mail-order company if you expect to make a fortune overnight.

53. Try to get the quality of sincerity into your sales letters. According to Billy Graham, considered one of this century's most effective communicators, "Sincerity is the biggest part of selling anything."

54. Realize that some of the big success stories in mail order have resulted from seeing a consumer need and filling it.

55. Try to develop more imagination. Imagination can sky-rocket your profits and income in mail order.

56. Subscribe to the *Gift and Decorative Accessories Buyer* magazine. It covers new items in the gift trade. The present address is 51 Madison Avenue, New York, New York 10038.

57. Start your mail-order business with small classified ads.

58. Sign all your outgoing letters. It creates a much better impression.

59. Don't let your age discourage you. Ray Kroc, the man behind the McDonald's restaurant success, didn't launch his McDonald's career until his middle 30s. He was past 40 before he became rich.

60. Write crisp, fresh copy for your ads. Make every word pull its weight.

61. Stick with a pulling ad until the returns from it begin to fizzle out.

62. Keep alert for items that will trigger repeat orders.

63. Use an order form built into your sales letter to save money.

64. Hold frequent brainstorming sessions with your mind. Try to come up with new product and advertising ideas that will make your business grow.

65. Learn how to type. It can be a great help in your business.

66. Key every ad that you run, so you can judge the pulling power of each publication and copy arrangement you use.

67. Practice writing sales letters until you feel confident that you can write a winner.

68. Keep a carbon copy of every business letter you send out.

69. Know at all times what your competition is offering.

70. Avoid offering heavy items, so the shipping expense won't eat up your profits.

71. Visit gift centers in large cities and gift shows whenever possible. You'll find that these visits will stimulate new ideas.

72. Realize that "Five times as many people read a headline as read the body of an ad," according to David Ogilvy, the veteran advertising expert.

73. Know that the family of the future will be smaller, but more mature.

74. Offer a manual on solar energy and its use in heating homes. This should be a steady mail-order seller for years to come.

75. Delay launching a catalog until you've gained considerable experience and have enough items to make it worthwhile.

76. Send a refund at once to anyone who requests it.

77. Use color in your direct-mail package (sales letter, order form, circular, and reply envelope) whenever possible.

78. Keep your advertising copy simple.

79. Don't buy catalogs from existing companies with your own company name imprinted on them. You can do better offering your own items.

80. Realize that the great creators and thinkers of history stood alone against the men of their time. Practically all new ideas were opposed.

81. Open your ad with a powerful headline that grabs attention.

82. Be alert for new ideas constantly.

83. Realize that most checks received with mail orders will be good.

84. Try to offer a variety of items by mail. But do it slowly and carefully.

85. Keep close tabs on the amount of stock you have on hand for each item. Be sure you can fill all incoming orders. But avoid overstocking any item that doesn't sell.

86. Realize that every great achievement came from the mind of some independent creator.

87. Treat all customers and prospects the way you'd like to be treated. The Golden Rule definitely applies to the mail-order business.

88. Try to select products and items that many people need.

89. Keep your customers informed about your new products or offers. They'll buy from you again and again.

90. Follow up on those who send you requests for details on an offer. If they don't send an order right away, try again later. Inquiry names have been sold on the twentieth and thirtieth attempts, so don't be too quick to give up on them.

91. Quote your asking price for low-priced items in round dollars.

92. Use a broker with a reliable reputation whenever you rent a mailing list. And ask questions about the nature and quality of the list. There are all kinds of lists floating around. You should use the best ones.

93. Know that wealthy people fail to show any special set of personality traits that make them different from ordinary people.

94. Be sure that every direct-mail package you send out includes a sales letter, order form, circular, and reply envelope.

95. Know that all mail-order publications are happy to send you free information on their current advertising rates.

96. Think about how William Lear originated the car radio, the Lear jet, the eight-track tape player, and over 150 other inventions. He often put in a 12-hour day—even at age 75.

97. Remember that the price range of products advertised in mail-order publications may vary widely. As an example, products currently advertised in *House Beautiful*'s "Window Shopping" section range from one or two dollars for a color brochure to $23 (for lace curtains) to $100 and $265 (for special kinds of tables).

98. Keep offering new items from time to time to your growing customer list. Many will buy from you again and again.

99. Do your best to fill all orders within 24 hours. This will help you build a list of satisfied customers.

100. Start out with a low-priced item if you want to. But try to sell a higher-priced offer as soon as you can, for it will be more profitable.

appendix II

Bibliography

Brabec, Barbara. *Homemade Money*. White Hall, Virginia. Betterway Publishers, 1984.

Braun, Irwin. *Building a Successful Pro Practice With Advertising*. New York: AMACOM, 1981.

Brumbaugh, J. Frank. *Mail-Order—Starting Up—Making It Pay*. Radnor, Pennsylvania: Chilton Book Company, 1979.

Burstiner, Irving. *Mail-Order Selling*. Englewood Cliffs, New Jersey: Prentice-Hall, 1982.

Cohen, William A. *Building a Mail-Order Business*. New York: John Wiley and Sons, 1982.

Crown, Paul. *Building Your Mailing Lists*. New York: Oceana Publications, 1973.

Foster, Robert E. *Business Mailer's Handbook*. Englewood Cliffs, New Jersey: Prentice-Hall, 1977.

Fryburger, Vernon. *The New World of Advertising*. Chicago: Crain Books, 1975.

Goldstein, Arnold S. *Starting on a Shoestring*. New York: John Wiley and Sons, 1984.

Goldstein, Sue. *The Underground Shopper*. Kansas City: Andrews and McMeel, 1983.

Hodgson, Richard S. *The Dartnell Direct Mail and Mail-Order Handbook*. Chicago: Dartnell Corporation, 1980.

Hogue, Cecil. *Mail-Order Moonlighting*. Berkeley, California: Ten Speed Press, 1976.

Iglesia, Maria Elena De La. *The Catalogue of Catalogues*. New York: Random House, 1975.

Kaufman, William. *The Mail-Order Food Book*. New York: Grosset and Dunlap, 1977.

Kishel, Gregory and Patricia. *Dollars on Your Doorstep*. New York, The Wiley Press, 1984.

Lowry, Albert J. *How to Become Financially Successful by Owning Your Own Business*. New York: Simon and Schuster, 1981.

Marcus, Stanley. His and Hers: *The Fantasy World of the Neiman-Marcus Catalog*. New York: Viking Press, 1982.

Ogilvy, David. *Ogilvy on Advertising*. New York: Crown Books, 1983.

Shilling, Dana. *Be Your Own Boss*. New York: William Morrow and Company, 1983.

Simon, Julian L. *How to Start and Operate a Mail-Order Business*. New York: McGraw-Hill, 1981.

Stern, Alfred. *How Mail-Order Fortunes Are Made*. New York: Arco Publishing Company, 1979.

Tilson, Ann and Weiss, Carol. *The Mail-Order Food Guide*. New York: Simon and Schuster, 1977.

Index